A BOOK OF BOOZE

BY THE SAME AUTHOR:

The Outsider Cycle

THE OUTSIDER

RELIGION AND THE REBEL

THE AGE OF DEFEAT

THE STRENGTH TO DREAM

ORIGINS OF THE SEXUAL IMPULSE

BEYOND THE OUTSIDER

INTRODUCTION
TO THE NEW EXISTENTIALISM

NEW PATHWAYS IN PSYCHOLOGY
Maslow and the Post-Freudian Revolution

A BOOK OF BOOZE

Colin Wilson

LONDON
VICTOR GOLLANCZ LTD
1974

ISBN 0 575 01831 3

Printed in Great Britain by
Ebenezer Baylis & Son Ltd.
The Trinity Press, Worcester, and London

For

Paul Griffiths

ACKNOWLEDGEMENTS

I wish to thank the following for help and advice: Dr Harold Phelps, Messrs P. D. Griffiths (of the Wine Society), George Rainbird, Dennis Watkins, David Pugh and Leonard Hibbs. Rudolph Nassauer read the chapter on German wine and made invaluable comments. I also owe a great deal to the criticisms of Raleigh Trevelyan. Mr Roald Dahl was kind enough to allow the lengthy quotation from his story 'Taste', from *Someone Like You*, published by Michael Joseph Ltd. My debts to other writers on wine—Alexis Lichine, William Younger, Maurice Healy, Edward Hyams, Cyril Ray, Raymond Postgate, Alec Waugh, Edmund Penning-Rowsell, W. E. Massee, Creighton Churchill—will be obvious to all who know their wine literature. And, like most of these writers I owe more than I can say to those two presiding geniuses of the literature, George Saintsbury and André Simon.

Gorran Haven, June 1973

CONTENTS

A BOOK OF BOOZE

INTRODUCTION

The Poetry of Wine

I HAVE BEEN a regular wine drinker ever since I could afford it—that is, since the publication of my first book in 1956. A brief calculation informs me that about 1,500 gallons have gurgled and cascaded down my throat since that time, and that if this wine was poured into the basement room where I am at present sitting, it would flood it to a depth of eighteen inches. It follows that if I live to be ninety, and continue at my present rate of consumption (around a bottle a day), I shall have drunk enough to drown in. An astonishing thought, which gives rise to speculations on how the human liver can survive such a deluge. Apparently it can, though. In the back of my copy of *The Curiosities of Ale and Beer* by John Bickerdyke, I find the following remarks in my own handwriting—apparently copied from some article on alcoholic beverages: 'No disease is directly caused by alcohol, although it can severely lower resistance. Cirrhosis of the liver, long assumed to be of alcoholic origin, is basically a protein and Vitamin B deficiency, exaggerated but not caused by excessive drinking; however much a man drinks, he has a ninety per cent chance of ending with a normal liver.' To which I add that real wine drinkers are seldom alcoholics, or even excessive drinkers; they enjoy it too much to treat it as an anaesthetic. The true alcoholic is concerned with quantity rather than quality, with the effect on the nervous system rather than on the palate.

There are two kinds of book about wine. One sets out simply to impart information. It may be short and simple, or positively encyclopedic; but its aim is to teach you about wine as if you were taking an exam. The other kind is intended to be read while you actually drink; that is, it is written by people who enjoy drinking wine, to convey their pleasure to the reader. They are as frankly personal and digressive as *The Essays of Elia*. My own favourites in this genre are Saintsbury's *Notes on a Cellar-Book*, Maurice Healy's *Stay Me with Flagons*, and Alec Waugh's *In Praise of Wine*. This present book is intended to belong to the latter rather than the former class. A friend who read the first chapter in manuscript objected that it contained rather more history than is necessary to understand the development of viticulture. This was obviously true; and I began tentatively to pencil out the irrelevancies. The resulting chapter so bored me that I put them all in again.

And if this book is to make a virtue of its irrelevancies, I may as well begin by explaining how my drinking gets done. I seldom drink during the day, for I find that it makes me drowsy. I write throughout most days, starting between 10 and 11 a.m. On warm summer days, I take periodic breaks to mow the lawns; this produces a feeling of virtue, and ensures that the tiredness I feel towards six o'clock is not entirely mental. In winter I work straight through the day, with the aid of large mugs of tea. At a quarter to six, I go upstairs, pour myself a drink, and watch the news. Nowadays I usually start with a glass of some dryish white wine. It may be a hock or Moselle, an Italian Soave, an Alsacien Riquewihr, or any dry French wine—I have a particular liking for the white wine of Rully, in the Côte Chalonnaise, which has a stronger flavour than Chablis. And I have no objection to a Jugoslav Riesling that our local brewery sells in gallon bottles. I keep this evening wine inside the door of the refrigerator, although the acknowledged authorities frown upon the practice. (Hilaire Belloc, who ought to know, once said there is no harm in drinking even a red wine cold; better a chilled burgundy than no burgundy at all.) If I am hungry, the white wine goes down well with a few anchovies on rye biscuits, or a little smoked salmon (if the children have left any). It is for drinking, not sipping; its purpose is to quench the thirst and induce relaxation.

After the news, I am ready for music, and for red wine. For everyday drinking, this is something light, and not too heady: an ordinary Beaujolais, or the Wine Society's Red Carafe, is my usual choice. When people first begin drinking wine regularly, they tend to switch from one wine to another; and also, to drink the best wine they have available. I know a well-to-do American who may be found drinking a *premier cru* claret or a vineyard-bottled burgundy at six in the evening—not because he is a wine fanatic, but because he feels he may as well drink the best he can afford. Such extravagance strikes the experienced wine drinker as a waste. The right time to drink a very good wine is with a very good meal. For everyday purposes, *vin ordinaire* is the right drink. And there is an important advantage in sticking to the same wine, once you have discovered one you enjoy: your system adjusts to it; and if, in the course of an absorbing conversation, you drink a glass or two more than usual, the ill effects are minimised. Not long ago, I called on a friend who had had the misfortune to break his leg, and we drank a bottle of Moulin à Vent between us, a Beaujolais that I find slightly heavy. When I came home, I drank half a bottle of the Society's Red Carafe, which is also a Beaujolais-type wine, pleasantly light-bodied. So the actual quantity I drank was the same as usual—that is, about one bottle in the course of an evening. Nevertheless, I woke up in the middle of the night with the kind of headache that comes from mixing your drinks, or drinking in a room full of cigarette smoke. (I am a non-smoker.) Clearly, my system prefers to deal with one wine at a time, and is indifferent to the argument that Beaujolais is Beaujolais, whatever the label.

I tasted wine for the first time when I was nineteen—I am not now counting the occasional mouthful of port at Christmas time as a child. I think it was George Orwell who remarked that if you want to decide whether a man is working class or middle class, you should ask him whether he has a bottle of sherry in the sideboard. The middle class home can usually produce a drink of some sort, if only cooking sherry. My home was decidedly working class, so Christmas was the only time when there might be a little alcohol on the premises. And when the Second World War started—I was eight at the time—even this ceased. I vaguely remember my grandfather allowing me to taste his port, and it seemed the most delicious drink in the world: warming, glowing, sweet, and with a smell that struck me as more poetic than autumn leaves or newly cut grass. One of the nicest things about being rich must be to be able to drink port every day. The names of drinks were evocative. Sherry and Brandy seemed to call up fairytale landscapes. (I can understand why Tolkien has a river called the Brandywine at the boundary of his Hobbit shire.) Whisky sounded adventurous, the kind of thing they would drink in the wild west. Gin sounded coarse, almost like a swearword. Beer sounded flat and unexciting. The most exciting of all was burgundy, perhaps because I associated it with *The Vagabond King*:

Sons of toil and danger
Will ye serve a stranger
And bow down to Burgundy?

At the age of nineteen, having succeeded in getting myself discharged from the RAF after six months' service, I crossed from Dover to Calais with less than a pound in my pocket. The dock area of Calais was still flat and bare, the result of bombing. I went into a grocer's and bought a loaf of bread, some cheese, and a kilo of onions. (I thought a kilo was half a pound, but lacked the courage to change my order.) Then I noticed the bottles of wine in the window at 100 francs each. That was only about two shillings in 1950. I bought one, and as soon as I reached an open country road, I sat down on the grass, pulled out the cork, and poured myself half a mug. The first mouthful tasted so awful that I spat it out. My first suspicion was that it had gone off—this obviously explained why it was so cheap. But since I had nothing else to drink to wash down my cheese and onion, I swallowed it. And after ten minutes, the world began to glow in a delightful manner. Nothing mattered any more. There was a feeling of being brimfull of warmth and vitality. I had no money, but I was in France, and life was all adventure, and the future undoubtedly meant well by me. I had often experienced this sensation in the past: when I first went to work in a factory at the age of 16, I used to deliberately induce it in the evenings by reading all my favourite poetry; but the wine made it stronger than ever before. After a while, a car stopped for me, and took me on towards Lille. I heard the driver say to his wife: '*Il est sou.*' But I wasn't. I was just feeling happier than I had felt in years. The feeling might be described as 'breathing-space'; the sensation that life has ceased to put pressure on you, and is suddenly allowing you to sit back and contemplate human existence as if you were *above* it.

It was some years after that first experience of burgundy before I could afford to explore the world of alcoholic beverages. I made two trips to France in the early 'fifties, and lived there a couple of months each time; but on neither occasion could I afford to buy wine, or even—what at the time interested me more—the delicious-looking cakes sold in French confectioners'. Between the ages of nineteen and twenty-four, I worked at any job the Labour Exchange offered me, and tried to write a novel, which eventually became *Ritual in the Dark*. There is a scene in *Ritual*, which dates from this period, in which the hero visits an empty basement flat to collect a bag of clothes; the flat belongs to a rich acquaintance, who tells him to help himself to a drink. He finds that the drink cupboard is full of liqueurs: Cointreau, Crème de Menthe, Benedictine, Kirsch, Tia Maria, and so on; he tastes a teaspoonful of every one until he is drunk. This was wishful thinking on my part; I used to look at all the liqueurs behind the counters in French bars, and think how delightful it would be to have enough money to try every one of them. That scene in *Ritual* was inspired by Huysmans's *A Rebours*—the 'organ' of liqueurs in the fourth chapter, on which Des Esseintes plays symphonies of taste, with crème de menthe as the flute, Curaçao the clarinet, Kümmel the oboe.

Huysmans is right: alcohol has its own important role in the life of the mind, like poetry and music. Its ultimate justification is to be found in such moments as the one I have described above, the 'breathing spaces'. Rilke once described how, leaning on a tree in a garden, he was overtaken by one of those moments of total stillness 'like the silence in the heart of a rose'. To me, such moments bring an extremely clear insight: that we possess ranges of power that are unknown to everyday consciousness. I have experienced it sitting in a pub in Mevagissey, near my home, waiting for the old judge with whom I used to drink in the early evenings. The window was wide open at the end of a hot summer day; the air had that cool, tired smell. The street was crowded with summer visitors, but the small bar was almost empty. I was drinking Beaujolais—bottled by Patriarche—but at that stage had not drunk more than half a glass. Suddenly, all my tensions seemed to be expelled in one long sigh, and Mevagissey became the most delightful place in the world. The same thing has often happened on holidays, especially at the end of a long day's driving. We would check in at a hotel; my wife would be left to do the unpacking and attending to the children; I would take a shower, change into fresh clothes, then make my way down to the bar—always carrying a book, which in practice I never read, because the strangeness of the surroundings, and the relaxation induced by the drink, produced alchemical changes in consciousness. I recall such a bar at Fort William in Scotland, with a long window overlooking Loch Linnhe. It was not a first-class hotel, and when we enquired about dinner, we were told we could have 'high tea' at half past six. And there was no wine—which we found to be the rule rather than exception in Scottish hotels at the time. But since this was Scotland, and there was a nip in the air, I had a large whisky. Possibly I had two. I cannot recollect the name of the whisky, or whether it was malt or blended; but I can still recall clearly that feeling of the opening up of inner space, as if some nasal blockage vanished, then went on widening, producing a floating sensation of freedom.

What has always fascinated me is the precise way in which such inner changes occur. Obviously, this is not purely a chemical reaction, for if I am feeling depressed, half a dozen whiskies may leave me gloomily sober. Neither is it simply a matter of relaxation, for under different circumstances, alcohol may relax me and make me dull and sleepy. The interesting thing about these experiences is that *ninety-five per cent* of my being relaxes, and the other five per cent stays wide awake. I can remember queueing outside cinemas as a child, willing to wait hours to see such renowned British epics as *The Seventh Veil* and *Odd Man Out*; and how, once inside, in the warm, soothing darkness, that smelt of cigarette smoke and ice cream, there was a marvellous sense of relaxation, like sinking into a feather bed, while at the same time the eyes were focused avidly on the screen, determined not to miss even the advertisements for local shops. Such hours, among the most enjoyable experiences I can call to mind from childhood, were characterised by what you might call 'controlled relaxation'—ninety-five per cent relaxation, five per cent intense concentration. Surely the same formula applies to the alcohol-induced moments I am describing? You sigh and relax, but a part of your attention remains alert, focused on the bottles and glasses, or on the fire in the grate. Perhaps some companion begins to tell you a commonplace story about the day's events, or where he intends to spend his next holiday, not subjects that would normally engage your full attention, but you fasten on what he is saying with a kind of gratitude, as if it is of deep personal interest. And in a sense it is, for the story serves as the focal point for the attention, while the rest of you sighs and relaxes. *This* is what drinking is all about.

This raises a fundamental point about the effect of alcohol: its power to release emotions that in less civilised ages found outlet in battle or adventure. H. B. Morton said of Hilaire Belloc that 'there were so many men mixed in him that his variety was inexhaustible', while the delightful Dixon Scott (who was killed in the First World War) said of Chesterton that he was too big for his books. These are more than conventional compliments: they touch something essential about both men. Belloc foot-slogged across France and Italy, and sailed his yacht the *Nona* around the coast of England; but his readers know that it was the wine and beer he drank en route that turned these voyages into adventures that freed the soul. As to Chesterton, there is a kind of violence at the heart of his best writing—although perhaps it is only the violence of a man who longs to turn somersaults and throw stones at dustbin lids.

'The village church was hewn out of ancient and silent stone, bearded with fungoids and stained with the nests of birds. And yet, when they saw it from below, it sprang like a fountain to the stars; and when they saw it, as now, from above, it poured like a cataract into a voiceless pit.'

What can such men *do* in our industrialised, mechanical civilisation? In retrospect, the tomfoolery in Chesterton's novels is tragic: the poet who stands on his head and waves his feet at the sky, the husband who rushes around the world for the pleasure of seeing his wife as if he has just met her. Yet a carafe of Beaujolais in a Fleet Street pub could transform tragedy into poetry, produce a glowing expansion of consciousness in which London ceased to be a City of Dreadful Night, and became as magical as the Emerald City of Oz.

'It was a quaint, quiet square, very typical of London, full of an accidental stillness. The tall, flat houses round it looked at once prosperous and uninhabited; the square of shrubbery in the centre looked as deserted as a green Pacific islet. One of the four sides was much higher than the rest, like a dais, and the line of this was broken by one of London's admirable accidents—a restaurant that looked as if it had strayed from Soho. It was an unreasonably attractive object, with dwarf plants in pots and long striped blinds of lemon-yellow and white.'

In a Graham Greene novel the restaurant would be scabrous and nasty, and the owner would be a chain smoker who bites his nails and dreams of nubile schoolgirls.

All this is not to say that wine is a magical potion, capable of scattering stardust over the everyday world; even applied to music, such a claim would be exaggerated. Wine acts upon the body and nervous system; its only certain effect is to anaesthetise you if you drink enough. The poets are inclined to pitch their claims too high. Belloc writes in his 'Heroic Poem in Praise of Wine':

Wine, true begetter of all arts that be;
Wine, privilege of the completely free;
Wine the recorder; wine the sagely strong;
Wine, bright avenger of slydealing wrong.

Here every sentence is a downright lie, except the last one, which is meaningless. Yet one can see what he is getting at: he is trying to say the unsayable, to express that absurd, ineffable feeling of the heroic that is sometimes induced by alcohol.

This also explains the high incidence of alcoholism among writers and artists—particularly since the onset of the Industrial Age, which is, by definition, anti-heroic. The writer has an inner-compass that seeks out the heroic as an ordinary compass seeks magnetic north. If he cannot find it, he is inclined to indicate south instead, and to complain about the meaninglessness of human existence. In that case, he may also become an alcoholic. Belloc and Chesterton were not alcoholics because they had imagination enough to construct a heroic mythology, which involved the Middle Ages, the Catholic Church and a nostalgic yearning for the simple life. Less optimistic spirits made do with the bottle. Negley Farson told me how he had called on Scott Fitzgerald in the twenties. Fitzgerald was writing at a tall desk, and Negley asked him why he preferred to write standing up. 'Because,' said Fitzgerald, 'when I sit down I start drinking that.' He pointed to a bottle of gin on the floor by the settee. Then he added: 'Come on, let's sit down'. The story makes me understand why *Tender is the Night* cost him such enormous efforts—and also why the book is so oddly depressing and nihilistic. It was so much easier to achieve the warm glow of inner-security and confidence from hard liquor than from hard writing. Fitzgerald knew the effort it cost him to write rather than drink; he assumed, mistakenly, that such writing must be superb. He wrote in a letter: 'It's good, good, good, and when they read it, they'll say it's good, good, good.' But it wasn't.

Fitzgerald also possessed that other necessary characteristic of the alcoholic: the ability to absorb large quantities of booze. When a New York doctor told Fitzgerald that he would die if he did not stop drinking, Fitzgerald agreed to ration himself to one gill of gin per day; he set out for home with a gill measuring glass in one pocket and a quart of gin in the other. On the way, he stopped off to see a friend; and then, sitting on the lawn, drank the bottle, gill by gill, as he talked. And when a friend called on him one day, Fitzgerald explained that he was not drinking, but mixed the friend a martini, after which he poured himself a glass of gin and downed it. Then he asked with mild surprise: 'Did I drink a glass of gin? I believe I did.' It could have been a joke, but the biographical evidence of this period of his life suggests that it was a genuine piece of absent-mindedness; drinking had become second nature.

The publication of *Tender is the Night*, with its obvious undercurrents of self-pity, led Hemingway to write Fitzgerald a typically brutal but honest letter, in which he told him: 'You're not a tragic character. Neither am I. All we are is writers.' He went on: 'Of course, you're a rummy. But you're no more of a rummy than Joyce is and most good writers are.' This was untrue. Joyce was not a 'rummy'—although he got drunk regularly—because he had inner resources, and his work would always be more important to him than his life. He would never lose himself in passive expectations of 'life' that were bound to be disappointed. And Hemingway himself was no rummy at this stage. The irony is that he became one later. And the reason that he became one was that his own pursuit of the heroic foundered. His early ideal was the man who can face up to life; who can swallow the bad things—with a wry face—and still enjoy the good things without prejudice. But it was always Hemingway's belief that too much thinking spoiled the directness of the experience. So as experience began to pall—as it will for the unreflective—he found himself relying increasingly on the gin bottle to release tensions. The 'portrait of the artist' that emerges in his last novel, *Islands in the Stream*, is of a man with no future, no development ahead of him, no new way to realise the heroic ideal that he has pursued through three wars and a dozen countries.

I have known a fair number of alcoholics, several of them writers. And in most cases (though not all) there was a tendency to personality change under alcohol. According to Sheila Graham, Fitzgerald became a kind of monster when he was drunk, becoming inconsiderate, loud-mouthed, boastful and belligerent. I have known a Celtic poet who was shy and monosyllabic when sober, but who could become relaxed and noisy and rather aggressive in ten minutes flat by downing a large whisky followed by Guinness. Come to think of it, I have known several Celtic poets like that; it seems to be a characteristic of the Scots and Irish.

On the island of Skye, I was introduced to a young man who wrote poetry, and plays in verse. He opened the conversation by saying he had read my books and thought they were no good. Since I showed no sign of being offended, he became friendly, and confided that he was the best living Scottish poet—in spite of Hugh McDiarmid, Norman McCaig, W. S. Graham and a few other contenders. I was impressed by his conviction, for I have always believed that all men of genius *know* they're good. He recited whole poems, full of Scots dialect, and they sounded magnificent. By the end of the evening, I was convinced I had met a potentially great writer. I saw him again the next morning, before we moved on; to my surprise, he was tongue-tied, and had a hang-dog look. I attributed this to a hangover—for I was suffering from the same thing. When I got back home to Cornwall, I wrote to him, asking him to send me the manuscript of a novel he had mentioned. After several weeks, I got a brief reply, saying that it wasn't yet ready. He didn't reply at all to subsequent letters. Then, rather belatedly, it dawned on me that he was an example of a phenomenon I have observed before: the Celt who becomes a cauldron of turbulent vitality after a couple of whiskies, then subsides into boredom and self-doubt when sober.

But I make this comment without cynicism. For this is no two-dimensional problem of self-deception. It would be *too* easy to dismiss my Celtic acquaintance as a moderately talented man who became convinced of his genius when a few drinks had diminished his capacity for self-criticism. But the opposite point of view is just as plausible: that he was a man of potential genius, whose habitual shyness and lack of confidence kept him below par. There are many such cases among men of acknowledged genius. Tchaikovsky wrote to his brother Anatole: 'I can't do without it. I never feel calm except when I have taken a little too much. I have so accustomed myself to this secret tippling that I feel a kind of joy at the sight of the [brandy] bottle . . . I can write letters only after a nip.' He used alcohol all his life to place himself in a relaxed state; but in the relaxed state, he wrote music.

There is a fundamental principle at stake here. The triviality of everyday life, its quality of meaningless repetition, keeps us in a state that is akin to hypnosis. It is like staring at a metronome. In moments of excitement or expanded awareness, we throw off the hypnotic trance. Meaning becomes self-evident. There is a Chaplin film in which the little drunk encounters a man of dual personality: affectionate and generous when drunk, mean and bad-tempered when sober. When I saw this film in my early teens, it struck me as being of symbolic importance. We all contain a Philip-Drunk and Philip-Sober. Philip-Drunk sees the world as a place of endless possibilities, a rising market in which any gamble will bring returns; Philip-Sober sees it as a confidence trickster trying to swindle him. Which one is right? There is no easy answer, but one thing is certain: Philip-Sober does not deserve to be right; he is a sluggard and a coward.

Our main trouble is our tendency to be bullied by our feelings; we accept them as infallible counsellors, and this is our downfall. The mistake arises by analogy with purely physical needs. I am hungry; I need food to refuel my vitality. I am cold; I need to get near a warm fire, or I may catch cold. I am tired; I had better rest to restore my energies. But then, if I feel depressed, I tend to accept this as a sign of some need that demands satisfaction; I respond by looking around for some form of self-indulgence. Perhaps I check to see if there's anything good on television. A woman may decide to go out and buy a new hat. I never consider the possibility that the depression may be a confidence trick. In fact, it usually is.

A friend—Hugh Heckstall Smith—told me a story about a dog that was subject to depressions. One day, looking in a cupboard, he accidentally locked the dog in. Five minutes later, he heard it scratching, and let it out; the dog bounded around joyously, all sign of depression gone. Hugh found it was an infallible method for combating the dog's depressions. When he saw it coming on, he locked the dog in the cupboard for five minutes; it always came out full of beans.

Our attitude towards life depends on how much we are *conscious of*—how many of its multiform possibilities are present to conscious awareness. Any serious threat or problem causes you to shake yourself into *deeper* awareness. Sudden pleasure or delight causes *heightened* awareness. In one case, consciousness is extended downwards, in the other, upwards. The interesting feature of alcohol is that it is the simplest chemical means we know for producing 'upward' awareness. There are plenty of other chemical means—drugs, for example—but their effect is cruder; most of them produce such a radical change in consciousness that it ceases to be consciousness of freedom. But the effects of wine are gentler and slower. If you are relaxed, and you *choose* to become conscious of your freedom (you may be watching television or listening to a conversation), you can control the gentle floating of the mind, as a glider pilot controls his craft on the air-stream. There is heightened awareness of your being ('who you are') and your possibilities. And at this point, the intelligent man uses his other faculties too: intelligence, imagination, memory. At this stage, alcohol is almost entirely a catalyst; its part in the heightening of awareness is gentle and unobtrusive.

All this explains the pleasure of understanding wine. There is more to *know* about wine than about any other form of alcohol. My wine library is not large—well under a hundred volumes—but I can spend weeks or months browsing through it without any sense of monotony. There are the histories of wine and the geographies of wine; the anthologies about wine—like the dozen volumes of *The Compleat Imbiber*; the general books about wine, like André Simon's *The Blood of the Grape*; and the particular books, like Cyril Ray's *Lafite*. Above all, of course, there are the autobiographical books, like Saintsbury's *Notes on a Cellar-Book*, Maurice Healy's *Stay Me with Flagons*, Alec Waugh's *In Praise of Wine*. Wine is like music; if your mind is half on something else, you miss the whole point. If I am listening to a piece of music I have never heard before, I want to know as much as possible about the music before I actually begin to listen. I look it up in Cobbett's *Cyclopedic Survey of Chamber Music*, in Grove, and in any other book that might carry a reference to it. And if I find a bottle of Chinon in a crate of mixed wines that I have purchased from the Wine Society for Christmas, I want to know more than the label tells me—that this is a red wine from the Loire. I want to know how the wines of the Loire differ from those of Beaujolais or the Rhône or the Côte d'Or, and why; so I begin by looking it up in Alexis Lichine's *Encyclopaedia of Wines and Spirits*, and then find out what André Simon, P. Morton Shand and Hugh Johnson have to say about it. It may seem a lot of fuss to make over a bottle of wine that cost me only 75p; but if I merely open it and drink it, I may fail to notice anything about it except that it is slightly more fragrant than a Beaujolais; with the help of the books as well as the wine, I make a brief voyage of the imagination, and return with some of the sense of refreshment we receive from a holiday.

ONE

On the Antiquity of Wine

WHEN THIS EARTH of ours was first formed, around five billion years ago, it was thousands of times bigger than its present size, and at least five hundred times heavier. But that was before the huge ball of gas we call the sun had contracted to a size where nuclear reactions began. The great, dark sphere turned a dull red, then into a dazzling furnace. Hot streams of ions swept the planets like a huge sand-blaster, tearing away the loose gas, and gradually reducing them to tiny, hot balls. Our earth cooled slowly; the water vapours condensed to form seas. And more than two billion years ago, the first tiny living organisms appeared.

What has all this to do with wine? Simply that these first organisms were very like the yeast that produces wine. They gobbled up the organic compounds that floated around them in the water, stole their energy, and then excreted simpler chemicals. Yeast does the same with the sugar in grapes, and the 'excretion' is alcohol. The gobbling process is called fermentation.

If space travellers ever land on a planet that resembles our earth of two billion years ago, they will find it a hot and inhospitable place. But it will have one great advantage. If they make wine, it will never go sour. On our planet, bacteria will carry on and convert the alcohol into acetic acid, and finally into carbon dioxide, ammonium salts and water. We stop this process by corking the wine in bottles, to keep out the oxygen. But on this primitive planet, there is no oxygen. It will appear later, as the cells develop the power called 'photosynthesis'—to take energy from sunlight, and use it to manufacture their own sugar. This must have happened fairly soon in the evolution of ilfe, otherwise these yeast-like organisms would quickly have 'gobbled up all the goodies' (as one physicist puts it) and starved to death. Some forms of photosynthesis released a poisonous gas called oxygen (poisonous to plants, that is); certain bacteria learned the trick of neutralising this poison gas by making it enter into combination with their 'excretion'. And that is precisely what happens to a bottle of wine if you leave it uncorked. It turns to vinegar.

It is an interesting thought, that when you drink any form of alcohol—wine, beer or spirits—you are drinking a by-product of the very earliest form of life; and if these forms had not continued to exist for two billion years, there would be no booze. Primitive life forms have their uses.

Since the reaction that turns fruit-sugar into alcohol is among the oldest of all chemical reactions on earth—and the simplest—it is probably safe to assume that the use of alcohol was discovered at a fairly early stage in human history. William Younger, in one of the most delightful histories of wine, *Gods, Men and Wine*, even speculates that it may have been known to men of the old Stone Age. Which raises the interesting question of how wine came to be discovered. William Younger quotes a story about the legendary hero-king of Persia, Jamshyd, who is supposed to have been fond of grape juice. One of his wives, in a suicidal mood, tried drinking from a jar of sour grape juice, which someone had labelled 'poison'. The poison made her pleasantly drowsy, and she woke up feeling better. So wine was discovered. . . . The obvious objection to this is that if the grape juice had 'gone off', it would have been thrown away, not labelled 'poison'.

It is this Jamshyd, incidentally, to whom Omar Khayyam refers:

> 'They say the Lion and the Lizard keep
> The courts where Jamshýd gloried and drank deep;
> And Bahrám, that great Hunter—the Wild Ass
> Stamps o'er his head, and he lies fast asleep.'

From which it is clear that Jamshyd transferred his allegiance from grape juice to its fermented form.

Younger, admitting that this is no more than a legend, insists nevertheless 'this is how wine must have been discovered'. Grapes would be kept in a pottery jar; the juice would run and ferment. One day, some bold man tasted the sour, sharp liquid. . . .

And then there is Maurice Healy, who (in *Stay Me with Flagons*) describes his own idea of how wine was discovered. Surely primitive man must have kept a store of grape juice to quench his thirst in summer? And surely there must have come a day when his wife made too much, and a forgotten jar began to bubble. 'One can imagine the curiosity with which primitive man and his wife watched this eager bubbling; one cannot but admire the courage of the first person to taste the juice when the bubbling had ceased. It must have seemed odd and unfamiliar; but the sickly-sweet taste of the grape juice had gone; this new liquid was rather sour, a little prickly, and more grateful to a thirsty throat than grape juice ever had been. . . .' But *would* 'primitive man' keep a store of grape juice to drink in summer? The working class household of my childhood was by no means 'primitive', yet we didn't even keep a bottle of lemonade in the larder for summer days; if we had, it would have been drunk within twenty-four hours. If we wanted a drink, there was water in the tap. There was never spare food and drink in the house, except at Christmas. And this, I would like to bet, applied to primitive man. What is more, even if some tribal chief kept jars of grape juice for his own use, nothing is less likely than that he watched the fermentation with interest, then had the courage to try it. Primitive men are not characterised by the urge to experiment; because they are fighting to retain what they have, they tend to be intensely conservative; the innovator runs the risk of being executed as a trouble-maker.

My own suggestion is that primitive man learned about the properties of alcohol when he was starving, and was forced to eat half-rotten fruit—just as, at the end of the winter, he must have been forced to eat half-rotten meat. Imagine a family of Stone Age hunters, around 20,000 B.C., at the end of a year of exceptionally bad weather, when rain and high winds have stripped leaves and fruit from the trees, and made hunting almost impossible. They are forced to eat what they can find—flyblown berries, half-rotten apples. There is an odd smell about the fruit; the skin is covered with white spots, and it has a sharp, fizzy taste. It produces diarrhoea, but also a curious feeling of light-headedness, of walking on air. . . . Stone Age man would note the effect, but prefer not to repeat the experiment, unless driven to it by necessity.

Seven or eight thousand years pass by; in south east Asia, Mesolithic man has discovered that certain plants can be domesticated. The grape was not among these—it did not exist in the southern hemisphere until man took it there—but barley and maize certainly were, and both can be fermented. So can honey, another staple food of primitive man. Recent archaeological discoveries in Vietnam and Thailand have shown that the age of farming began there some five thousand years before it appeared in Mesopotamia, previously regarded as 'the cradle of civilisation'. At this period, they had no pottery, so the storing of liquids would have presented difficulties. But now the family has ceased to be nomadic, the storage of fruit and grain for the winter becomes one of the main tasks of the women; if no one had noticed the heady properties of fermented fruit before, they must have done so now. In that case, we might assume that the invention of alcoholic drink followed fairly close on the invention of pottery.

In his 'social history of wine', *Dionysus*, Edward Hyams discounts the suggestion of Russian authorities that wine may have been invented as early as 8000 B.C. But that was written before the discovery of the early farming communities of south-east Asia*, when it was accepted that farming was invented about 8000 B.C. Now we know enough to suggest that mead and beer may have been known as early as 10,000 B.C. And the Russian guess of 8000 B.C. for the invention of wine may well be accurate; once fermentation had been discovered, every variety of juice would be tried. To begin with, its use was probably restricted to religious ceremonies—to induce ecstasy in tribal *shamans*, to create excitement in ritual dances. By the time of the first written records of civilisation, approximately 4000 B.C., the use of wine was taken for granted. After this date, there are many references in Egyptian pyramid texts to wine; so many that it was clearly an important part of civilised life in Egypt.

* See 'An Earlier Agricultural Revolution' by Wilhelm G. Solheim, *Scientific American*, April 1972.

An inscription on the tomb of Ptah-Hotep, who lived in Memphis around 4000 B.C., shows the processes of wine-making. There are pictures that show the grapes being gathered in baskets, and pictures that show them being trodden in a great vat, and the juice gushing out of the spout into a lower vat. The Egyptians also crushed the grapes with a device like a long tube of raffia-work, with a handle at either end; the grapes were placed inside it, and the handles were twisted in opposite directions, so the juice ran out through the raffia. The idea, of course, is to prevent the seeds of the grape from being crushed, for they would impart a bitter flavour to the wine. When this juice had fermented, and the impurities had been strained off, the wine was kept in tall jars—the Greeks called them amphoras—with a narrow neck that could be sealed with a clay plug.

One thing is fairly certain. Primitive man did not drink because he liked the taste of wine or mead. If he was interested in the taste, he would have preferred unfermented grape juice, or honey in warm water. His methods were primitive; his storage jars were porous, so the wine probably tasted of vinegar more often than not. He added sugar and various spices to his wine to make it palatable, while Younger records that in Babylonia and Homeric Greece, wine thickened with flour was regarded as especially palatable: simultaneously food, drink and intoxicant. Like the hero of Charles Jackson's *The Lost Weekend*, ancient man did not drink for the taste, but 'for what it did to him'.

After the invention of wine came beer. It must have come later, for the making of beer is a more complicated process than the making of wine. It was almost certainly discovered by bakers—who would handle grain in quantity—and for many centuries, the baker and the brewer were the same man. Beer is made from malt—that is, from a grain cereal (usually barley) which is soaked in water, then allowed to 'shoot', then dried out. The malt is ground into a flour, and made into a 'mash' with water. (In Germany, a jug of beer-mash which is more than 1,500 years old has been dug up.) It is heated and stirred, and the solids allowed to settle; the remaining liquid is called wort. Yeast is added to the wort; it ferments, and the result is beer. Nowadays we use hops to give this beer its character and flavour—they have been in use since the fourteenth century—but the Egyptians and Babylonians drank the rather insipid-tasting barley brew. In fact, beer soon became so popular that it replaced wine in their countries as the national drink. It was easier and cheaper to make than wine, less intoxicating. Wine continued to be used for religious purposes, but the really popular drink was beer—the Egyptians called a party a 'house of beer'. And beer also came to be used for pouring a libation to the gods, and for offerings to the dead, placed in Egyptian tombs.

It was not long before beer drinking became something of a social nuisance. Inevitably, perhaps. Life was savagely hard in ancient Egypt or Mesopotamia; you had to keep running to stay in the same place. The relaxation and detachment induced by beer must have seemed a foretaste of heaven to overworked husbandmen. But, from the point of view of the lawgivers and guardians of society, the taverns were centres of corruption. In Babylonia, beer houses and wine shops were usually run by women ('mine hostess' is an old tradition—perhaps, as Hyams says, because beer houses were originally brothels), and they were looked down upon as the haunt of the morally degraded. Around 2000 B.C., both Babylonia and Egypt went through a kind of prohibition crisis, and there was talk of closing all the taverns. The poor must have regarded this as horribly unjust; their diet was dreary enough: bread, dates, onions, oil, an occasional fish, cheese that was little more than curdled milk. The chief objection to the wine shops was that drunken people got into fights. Younger records a curious Assyrian law from the second millennium B.C., to the effect that a woman who has crushed a man's testicle in an affray should lose her finger; and if she has crushed both his testicles, she should also lose her nipples. It seems an odd state of affairs when a country should need to pass such a law; it seems to imply that the twisting of testicles was a common form of assault, and that women were as likely to be involved in brawls as men. And this immediately conjures up a clear picture of an Egyptian or Babylonian beer house of 2000 B.C., something like the Whitechapel of Jack the Ripper, with half-starved, toothless bawds watching their opportunity to pick a pocket. And since the men wore loin cloths or smocks, their most vulnerable part became accessible....

But then, it is inevitable that, in primitive countries, with enough civilisation to produce real dirt and squalor, alcohol should become the chief escape-hatch. What else was there? Religion—but then, for religion to offer a comfort comparable to alcohol, it needs an element of revivalist enthusiasm. The religion of Egypt and Babylon in 2000 B.C. was already ancient, ritualistic and remote. So alcohol came to play the same part in the ancient world that psychedelic drugs play in modern America.

Which raises one of the basic questions about alcohol, and its relation to civilisation. The great conquering peoples, from the ancient Persians to the Mohammedans, have been teetotallers. Herodotus mentions that the earliest Persians never drank wine; these were the wild horsemen who swept across the decadent kingdom of the Medes, and went on to establish the greatest of the ancient empires. Exposed to civilisation and easy living, the Persians became more decadent than the people they had conquered; they became the chief cultivators of the vine in the ancient world—and their empire was destroyed by the Greeks and the Macedonians.

The same problem appears in a more complex guise in Greece. It is there that we can see the conflict between the two great basic urges in man: the desire to subdue reality, and the desire to escape into a world of dreams and fictions. The artistic element came from the original inhabitants of the Aegean lands, the builders of the Minoan civilisation of Crete and the Mycenaean civilisation of the Peloponnese. These Aegean Greeks were overrun by invaders from the north, a kind of early Viking, harsh, barbaric, puritanical, and not particularly artistic. It was the third wave of invaders, the Dorians (who came between 1100 and 1000 B.C.), who imparted the sober eye-to-business of the Greek character. And it was the combination of these two strains that produced men like Euripides, Socrates and Plato. Left to itself, the barbarian temperament is infertile, the artistic temperament is decadent. It is the combination of the two that produces intellectual greatness.

Greek civilisation began in Crete: it is now known as Minoan, after the legendary King Minos; it was flourishing in 2000 B.C. Their wall-paintings and pottery show them to have been emotional, artistic, sensuous, and they enjoyed beer and wine. Around 1500 B.C., the nearby island of Santorin exploded; its volcano belched hot lava, then collapsed so the sea ran in, producing the effect of several hydrogen bombs. This was the beginning of the end for Cretan civilisation, which seems to have lost a large part of its navy—on which it depended for commerce. The barbarians took advantage of their weakness to invade. After the downfall of Cnossos—the Minoan capital—the city of Mycenae became the cultural centre of Greece: this was on the mainland, and its great palace is one of the wonders of archaeology. The Mycenaeans were also artistic; Agamemnon—of Homeric fame—ruled the city in the 12th century B.C. On the south coast lay Pylos, ruled by King Nestor, who also figures in Homer. Archaeological investigations at Nestor's palace have revealed huge wine jars, each one holding fifty gallons. Homer mentions that when Telemachus visited Nestor, he was served sweet wine that was eleven years old. (This may have been the very dark wine from Maronea, in Thrace, which Odysseus used to intoxicate the Cyclops.) And again, when Telemachus visits Menelaus in Sparta, he finds his host presiding over a feast; the name of the wine is not mentioned, but the taste must have been strong enough to disguise the drug that Helen slips in 'to melt sorrow and sweeten gall'. Homer mentions strings that held the lid of Nestor's wine jar, which seems to suggest a pottery lid sealed with clay, then held in place with strings.

These visits occurred after the fall of Troy (which occurred about 1184 B.C.). The civilisation of Odysseus and Menelaus was swept away about a century later by the tide of barbaric Dorians; the iron age replaced the bronze age, and there was no more feasting in the halls of Sparta. For in Lacedaemonia (where Sparta was situated), the older Greeks became 'helots' (or slaves) of their conquerors, and were treated with a harshness that brings to mind the Jews of Russia or Nazi Germany. To the north, where Athens sprang up, this barbarian element was absorbed; the result was what we now call 'the Greek genius'. The contrast between the Athenians and the Spartans has always fascinated historians, and deserves some comment here. For it must be remembered that the Athenians themselves had a streak of puritanism. They drank for pleasure, but they drank their wine mixed with water—two parts of wine to five of water. (Homer mentions that the priest Maron drank his Maronean wine mixed with twenty parts of water—a proportion that would reduce it to less than 1 per cent alcohol.) A member of the Areopagus—the Athenian legislative council—could lose his job if he paid a visit to a tavern. Plato suggested that men should not be allowed to drink until they were past the age of forty, when the alcohol might revive 'the delights of youth'. But the combination of speculative intelligence and austerity produced great art and literature. The Spartans were puritanical and militaristic; they valued discipline above all else. It sounds dreary enough; yet in many ways, the Spartans are more interesting than the easy-going, clever Athenians. Their daily life sounds so extraordinary and alien to us that it might have been invented by a science-fiction writer. The fully privileged citizens of Sparta were all nobles, surrounded and maintained by their helots, like the plantation owners of America's Old South, except that there were no 'poor whites'. These slaves were carefully watched, and if any among them showed signs of talent or leadership qualities, he was simply destroyed. Inevitably, this produced a fall in their genetic quality. At an earlier period, the Spartans seem to have appreciated poetry and music, which was exclusively military. But artists evolve, and as they evolve, they become more complicated. The old military music and military virtues cease to satisfy the spirit. As soon as their poets showed signs of decadence (around the sixth century), poets and musicians were banned; the Spartan lords muttered 'the old tunes are the best', and stuck to their marches.

The males lived communally, and ate at a mess table; they had no family life. The women were trained in athletics from childhood; they stripped for processions and ceremonies, and the young men were spectators of their rituals; it was all singularly sexless and high-minded. When the time came for young men to marry, there was a ritual seizing of the bride, as if she were being kidnapped. There was no honeymoon; the girl lost her virginity, and the young man went back to barracks. The girl then cut her hair short and wore men's clothes, to indicate that she was now playing an equal part with her husband in the service of the state. Unhealthy babies were killed by exposure; it was regarded as illogical to take the trouble to breed horses, and to allow the continuance of the race to depend upon chance. Oddly enough, the baby was washed in wine before it was examined to determine whether it could be allowed to live. Until they were seven, children were brought up by their mothers and helot nurses; after that, they became members of a 'herd', where they were drilled in toughness: fighting, wrestling naked, proving their courage by bearing pain without flinching. At twelve, each boy passed into the care of an older youth, whose business was to teach him. In spite of their stringent sexual morality, the Spartans apparently regarded these relationships—usually erotic—as perfectly normal and desirable. The elder boy's job was to educate his charge in the mental, physical and moral sense; if the boy cried out when fighting, his lover was punished. The boy had to learn to answer questions in the briefest possible way—the word laconic is derived from Laconia. When old enough, he entered the army, and the same harsh training continued; Plutarch's account of it makes it sound like the asceticism of mediaeval monks. He 'came of age'—as a citizen—at thirty, and could then play his part as a citizen. Since he was one of the idle rich, it might be assumed that the iron discipline would now relax, and he would become something of a playboy, like Wodehouse's Bertie Wooster. It is true that he spent his day at clubs; but keeping fit continued to be the chief preoccupation, and indulgence in family life would have been regarded as a sign of moral breakdown.

All this produced a singularly stable state, that lasted for centuries. Arnold Toynbee points out that the position of women was by no means as bad as it sounds; since the children were brought up virtually without fathers, the mother was the most important member of the family; in its final, decadent stages, Sparta became something like a matriarchy. This stability was bought at a high price: intellectual and artistic stagnation, a rigid life that sounds to us almost inhuman. The only thing that could touch the deepest springs of moral enthusiasm in the Spartan was the idea of his country. But this was something he shared with the rest of the Greeks, whose patriotism about their city-states (*polis*) was so intense that it was almost a form of religious fanaticism. This is an interesting point, in view of the realisation, in recent years, of the importance of the 'territorial urge' in men and animals: the fact that an animal, deprived of its territory, loses its moral backbone. The Greeks achieved their intellectual and artistic eminence because 'territory' was almost their religion. This is the real significance of those heroic stories of Marathon and Thermopylae and Salamis; they are the Greek equivalent of the Old Testament stories of men sacrificing themselves for their God.

All this enables us to understand the Greek attitude to wine. Because it was regarded as something of a disgraceful self-indulgence, they drank it well diluted. They drank wine flavoured with resin—called retsina—which to the northern European palate tastes like disinfectant, and it is generally explained in books on wine that the Greeks had to cure their wine skins with resin, so they had to get used to the taste; they also added resin as a preservative. But the Greeks also flavoured their wine with sea water, and apparently enjoyed this nauseating mixture (which must have produced nightmarish hangovers). All this seems to suggest that the Greeks had a somewhat ambivalent attitude to wine.

We must, of course, take into account that life in ancient Greece was hard; most people lived in poverty. The only alcoholic drink most workers could afford was a kind of imitation wine made by soaking grape skins in water, or adding water to the lees in the wine vat when the wine had been run off. In view of all this poverty, who could be surprised that the Greek philosophy advocated moderation in all things?

And now we come to one of the strangest episodes in the history of wine—the arrival of the god Dionysus, or Bacchus. Oddly enough, the books on wine have little to say about him, or what they have to say is purely historical and invites skipping. He was the god of wine, the result of one of Zeus's extra-marital affairs—this one with Semele, daughter of King Cadmus, founder of Thebes. (Cadmus had bad luck with Zeus; his sister

Europa was carried off by Zeus in the form of a bull.) He was torn to pieces several times, but was always restored to his former shape. His mother, Semele, was tricked into begging her mysterious lover to appear to her in his real form; Zeus appeared as lightning, and consumed her; but the unborn Dionysus was saved, and sewed up in his father's thigh until ready to emerge into the world. . . . The legends seem to make so little sense that it is tempting to treat them as archaic absurdities whose meaning has been lost.

To understand the true significance of Dionysus, it is necessary to see him in relation to his opposite, Apollo. All the writers on mythology are agreed that Apollo is the embodiment of the Greek spirit. J. C. Stobart says of him (in *The Glory that was Greece*): 'Apollo is the most virile god on Olympus, as he is the representative god of the most manly race in Hellas, the Dorians. [This should not be taken to mean that Apollo came to Greece with the Dorian invasion; he was there long before.] Study this god. If you can love him you will have learnt the secret of Dorian greatness. He is very simple, serious and severe; he has the asceticism of a good athlete who knows what discipline means for the sake of his club or country.' Apollo is the embodiment of the Greek virtues. And since Sparta was the chief Dorian state, we can think of Apollo as essentially the god of Spartan virtues. He is the god of light and of the sun.

Apollo is prominent in the *Iliad*—fighting, naturally, on the side of the Greeks. Dionysus is mentioned in the *Iliad*, but not as the god of wine; neither is he one of the Olympic pantheon. Homer speaks of him as 'raging', and this would seem to indicate that Homer knew of him as one of the dark gods from the north, worshipped with savage orgies. In fact, Dionysus seems to have originated in Thrace, the wild land that is now the northern part of Turkey. We know nothing about his origins, except that he was worshipped in the form of a bull, and that the worship was violent, involving sacrifice of an animal (or even a child) by tearing it to pieces. Frazer, in *The Golden Bough*, remarks that the 'rude tribes of Thrace' were 'notoriously addicted to drunkenness', and adds of the Dionysian cult: 'Its mystic doctrines and extravagant rites were essentially foreign to the clear intelligence and sober temperament of the Greek race.'

But what were these 'mystic doctrines and extravagant rites'? Frazer does not say, and probably had no idea. A sexual element certainly entered into them—in spite of Edward Hyams's denial that the orgies were sexual; why, otherwise, was Dionysus often symbolised as an erect phallus? Even the much later images of Dionysus bear traces of his sexual origin: they were in the shape of an armless pillar surmounted by a bearded head, or an upright post. He was a fertility god, associated—naturally—with fruit and trees, and Frazer mentions that two of the epithets applied to him were 'teeming' and 'bursting'—both with obvious sexual connotations. It is even significant that he was symbolised by a bull. Zeus produced Apollo (and his sister Artemis) by masquerading as a swan and seducing Leda; and Apollo, the god of sunlight, could well be symbolised by a swan, magnificent and white, floating above the earth. Seducing Semele, the mother of Dionysus, Zeus appeared as a mortal man; but he destroyed her as thunder and lightning; and he carried off her aunt, Europa, in the form of a bull. Again, the symbols are of sex and violence.

And when this religion of Dionysus finally reached Greece, sometime in the seventh century B.C.—that is, the century after Homer—it spread like a forest fire, meeting violent opposition from the older religion, but always, eventually, conquering. He had already met with opposition in Thrace, according to the legend; Lycurgus, a Thracian king, denied the divinity of Dionysus; the god drove him mad, so that he killed his own son with an axe (thinking he was pruning a vine), after which the king was seized by his own subjects, and torn to pieces by wild horses. Euripides's last play, *The Bacchae*, dramatises another Dionysian legend: how Dionysus returned to his birthplace, Thebes, where his cousin Pentheus was on the throne. Pentheus, understandably, was unwilling to acknowledge a blood-relative as a god, perhaps influenced by his aunts, who were of the opinion that Semele's story of being seduced by a god was pure invention to hide an ordinary love affair. Dionysus thereupon causes his 'madness' to settle on his aunts, who rush out on to the mountains and dismember live animals in their frenzy. When Pentheus goes to see what they are doing, his own mother tears him apart, believing that he is a lion. It is a strange, Nietzschean play. Euripides wrote it at the end of his life, when he had left Greece in disillusion, to go to Macedonia; he probably witnessed the orgiastic rites of the god there. And it seems possible that this typical humanist, this advocate of intellectual balance and scepticism, had the flexibility of spirit to respond with enthusiasm to this Hellenic form of Wagnerism. Not all commentators agree about this. Philip Vellacot argues that Dionysus is 'not one that decent people will be prepared to worship'*, and that the play 'deals with the danger to society arising from the cult of mass-emotion'; i.e., that Euripides recognised the Dionysian religion as a kind of primitive Nazism. He states that the god's 'inhuman cruelty arouses nothing but horror'—forgetting that the Greeks had stronger stomachs than we have. At all events, *The Bacchae* is one of the most powerful artistic expressions of the power of the god of the irrational.

And why did the religion of Dionysus sweep across Greece, until he had to be accepted as one of the gods of Olympus, even invading the sanctuary of Apollo at Delphi? Surely *because* the Greeks were so obsessed with 'moderation in all things'. Can anyone read about the life of Sparta without shuddering and thinking 'Rather them than me'? One of the most puzzling things about Dionysus is that he is not represented as some bearded forest satyr, a gleeful drunken Silenus, but as an effeminate, beardless youth dressed in silken garments. In *The Frogs*, Aristophanes pokes fun at him; he enters disguised as Hercules in a lion skin, and the real Hercules almost ruptures himself laughing at him. Aristophanes seems to feel about him rather as W. S. Gilbert felt about Bunthorne and other 'aesthetic' young men. Why did this distinctly effeminate god have such appeal to women? Not simply because he represented an escape from the kitchen sink. But because he represented an escape from the dreary, masculine ideals that oppressed them. Apollo had become the god of stupid soldiers and brainless patriots; Dionysus represented the artist, with his half feminine nature. He did not demand to be worshipped exclusively: only that his worshippers should pay him homage in the proper season.

We do not know much about the Dionysian orgies, but we

* *The Bacchae and Other Plays*, Penguin.

know they involved music as well as wine, and that the dancing became increasingly frenzied, until the worshipper had achieved complete abandonment, *ecstasis*. A follower of the psychologist Reich would probably argue that Greek women hardly knew what it was to achieve orgasm, and that their Dionysian festivals quite simply channelled their frustrated sexual energies. This is undoubtedly an oversimplification, but it probably contains an important element of truth. It is true that man lives by discipline, by 'facing up to' problems, by calculation and compromise and logic. But he *evolves* through the expression of emotion, by purging himself of desires by acting them out. All poets know this. 'Sooner murder an infant in its cradle than nurse unacted desire' says Blake, and many of his other comments make the same point: 'Exuberance is beauty' (a pure Dionysian proverb), 'Expect poison from standing water', 'The reason Milton wrote in fetters when he wrote of Angels and God, and at liberty when of Devils and Hell, is because he was a true Poet and of the Devil's party without knowing it'. In Blake's sense, Dionysus is the devil, as well as being the god of intoxication and life worship.

All this makes it sound as if Dionysus is merely the natural counterpart of Apollo, the romantic as opposed to the classical, undisciplined feeling opposed to form. This would be shallow. Dionysus and Apollo may have ended by sharing Delphi; in practice, there is no reconciliation. There is something fundamentally contradictory about the nature of Dionysus. It is illustrated in Gorki's amusing story of Tolstoy. As Tolstoy and Gorki were walking along the street, they saw two hussars striding towards them in their bright uniforms. Tolstoy said: 'Just look at them—military idiots, walking along like mechanical toys.' Then, as the soldiers walked past them, striding in perfect step: 'My God, aren't they magnificent!' Here we can see a phenomenon which I have called 'dual-value response'. Tolstoy's first set of values—civilised, humanistic, logical—is suddenly replaced by another set that seems to contradict them; and he is capable of responding to both sets of values *at almost the same moment*. You seldom find dual-value response in moralists and logical philosophers. Bertrand Russell is all of a piece; he would have continued to call them military idiots as they walked past him, and he would have thought this was admirable consistency. As far as his writing goes, the later Tolstoy is a single-value moralist; so is George Eliot; so is Ibsen. There is a kind of logical consistency in their ideas and opinions; they run from A to Z like a piano keyboard. In Blake and Nietzsche, there is a great gap in the middle of the keyboard; on one level, they can be as logical and humanistic and rational as Bertrand Russell; on another, they recognise an irrational force that contradicts the values of civilisation. 'The will to war is a higher will than the will to peace', wrote Nietzsche, and 'Will, pure will, without the troubles and perplexities of intellect—how happy, how free!'

And what is the significance of these reflections in a book on wine? They indicate the importance of alcohol in civilisation: they make clear, for example, what the American prohibitionists failed to take into account when they passed the Volstead Act. Logic is a vital part of human existence, but it can be treacherous. Because a person sees the world through the eyes of logic, he imagines he is seeing it truly, and in the only possible way. It is a kind of logic that makes men decide to commit suicide. It is logic that makes some of Chekhov's plays end with a shot offstage. But it is the opposite of logic that makes Chesterton's heroes decide to turn a somersault or go and sit on the roof; it is a direct impulse of life. Tolstoy is one of the few novelists who has caught this paradoxical life urge in a symbol. On his way to visit the Rostovs, Prince Andrew passes a dead-looking oak tree. ' "Spring, love, happiness", this oak seemed to say, "Are you not weary of that stupid, meaningless, constantly repeated fraud?" ' And Andrew thinks 'Yes, the oak is right . . .' That night, he overhears two girls talking at their bedroom window in the moonlight, and goes to sleep oddly disturbed. When he passes by the same oak the next day, it has burst into leaf, and is completely transfigured; Andrew experiences 'an unreasoning springtime feeling of joy and renewal'. It is this irrational springtime feeling of joy and renewal that is left out of account by logic; but not by Dionysus. If man is to evolve, he must be transported out of the stable, horizontal perspectives of his logic. Euripides could have described with accuracy the outcome of Prohibition in America:

convulsions, bloody violence, the release of a tide of lawlessness that still shows no sign of receding. Dionysus symbolises one of the deepest realities of the human condition; we ignore him at our peril.

No one knows what happened to the Greek genius after the time of Plato and Euripides. But it evaporated. A minor quarrel between Athens and Sparta flared into the Peloponnesian war, which dragged on for twenty-seven years, from 431 B.C. A great plague destroyed a quarter of the population of Athens, including its leading statesman and general, Pericles; finally, the war ended in the total defeat of Athens and the demolition of its walls. Perhaps military defeat destroyed the literary and philosophic genius of the Greeks; or perhaps that fine balance between the Dorian and Aegean elements in the Greek character —the will-drive of the Dorians and the artistic sensibility of the Aegeans—toppled over into decadence. In a modern Greek writer like Kazantzakis, the genius is distinctly un-Hellenic; there is a feeling of barbaric violence which is as far removed as possible from the spirit of moderation in all things; it is as if the Dorian has finally triumphed.

In the century that followed the Peloponnesian war, it looked for a while as though Greek culture might spread across Asia as well as Europe; Philip of Macedon—that savage country in which Euripides had witnessed the rites of Dionysus—regarded himself as a Greek, and proposed to lead the Greeks against Persia. Philip was assassinated, but his son Alexander carried out the plan. When Thebes attacked him, he destroyed it; then he beat a Persian army, built himself a city in Egypt—called Alexandria—and went on to conquer Persia and take over its eastern empire. He was thinking of adding Africa to his empire when he died at thirty-three.

It is conceivable that his early death was one of the great tragedies of world history. If Alexander had lived to reign over his empire, the culture of the Greeks—which he had learned from his tutor Aristotle—might have spread over the ancient world, from Alexandria to Samarkand and Karachi. The possibilities of inter-cultural fertilisation would have been tremendous. But when Alexander died, the empire broke up.

From our point of view, the chief interest of the idea of a long-lived Alexander is the possibility of a wine empire stretching from Egypt to India and southern Russia. For as early as the sixth century B.C., the Greeks were the great wine traders of the Mediterranean; even Egypt bought its wine from them. Persia had its own wine (as already noted, the legendary inventor of wine, King Jamshyd, was a Persian); but the Persians lacked the Greek finesse on the subject of viticulture. Beer was their national drink; in fact, legend declares that Dionysus originated in Persia, but left in disgust because the inhabitants preferred beer; when the Persians drank, they drank to get drunk. (Herodotus records an interesting Persian custom of taking all important decisions when drunk, and reflecting on them the next day when sober.) The Greeks trained and pruned their vines, and made an art of wine-making; the Persians left their vines unpruned, and their general attitude suggests that they didn't care what the wine tasted like so long as it was potent.

But Alexander died. And the seat of power in the ancient world moved from Greece to Rome. For several centuries, Carthage—on the North African coast—was also a contender—until the Romans burned it to the ground and ploughed the ashes into the soil in 146 B.C.

School history books give the impression that Rome was built centuries after Athens; in fact, it probably came into existence at about the same time—in the seventh or eighth century B.C.—as a small agricultural town or collection of villages. To the north of them flourished the culture of the Etruscans, who came from Asia Minor; there may even be some truth in the legend that they were originally Trojans, fleeing after the destruction of Troy.

Although curiosity about the Etruscans dates back as far as the Emperor Claudius—who was also a historian—they remain a historical mystery. D. H. Lawrence found them fascinating because their art glows with a delight in the physical world; a strong feeling of gaiety flows from early Etruscan wall paintings; they enjoyed eating and drinking, hunting and love-making, dancing and singing. Athenaeus, in the *Deipnosophist*, describes their orgies. The luxury of their way of life was a by-word. They lacked prudish feelings on the subject of nudity; naked boys and girls waited at table; one ancient historian—Timaeus of Taormina—says that their children never knew who their fathers were. Paintings show them drinking wine, but we know as little about this as about their customs and language. All we *do* know is that the Etruscans and the Romans clashed, but as the Romans slowly rose to power, the Etruscans became their subjects, and later Etruscan art indicates that the gaiety vanished, to give way to a certain gloomy stoicism.

The early history of Rome is a struggle between the patricians, who ruled, and the plebeians, who laboured and fought in the army. Slowly, the plebeians gained their political rights, and Rome became a kind of democracy. This was the foundation of its power; it was governed by its ablest and most energetic men. They extended the same privileges—of citizenship—to neighbouring tribes, with the result that they built up an enormous credit balance of loyalty. It was this loyalty that saved Rome when the Carthaginian Hannibal crossed the Alps with his armies and elephants; for although Rome lost the battles, Hannibal found he could gain no support from the rest of Italy; these tribes were free citizens of Rome, not slaves awaiting liberation. It was the loyalty they inspired, as much as their military prowess, that made Rome a great empire.

There was one sense in which the Romans were superior to the Greeks; they were more stable, more level-headed, more determined; they were rather contemptuous of the Greeks for wasting so much time squabbling amongst themselves. They even had the good sense to absorb Greek culture—which meant taking over Greek methods of wine-making as well as the Greek gods. And the vine proved an invaluable civilising influence in the barbarian lands that became part of the Roman Empire. They planted vines in Spain, in Germany, in Gaul (although the Greeks were responsible for planting vines in Marseilles). The savage tribes of Germany were a thorn in the side of the Romans. They would rush from their dark forests, slaughter a legion, and vanish again. Rome would send out more legions to teach them a lesson; barbarians were crucified, and heads and hands were chopped off. The savages would agree to accept the might of Rome—and then, two years later, rise up and slaughter another Roman legion. . . . It became tiresome, until some inspired peacemaker thought of encouraging them to grow vines along the wide, sunlit valleys of the Rhine and the Moselle. The belligerent savage discovered that well-tended vines produce plentiful grapes, and that the wine pressed from them can lighten the burden of existence. He also made the interesting discovery that some slopes produce better grapes than others, and that the wine from different vineyards may taste as different as if it came from another country. It was now no longer in his interest to slaughter the Romans and take to the forest; he might lose his best vineyards. . . . And so wine proved to be a civilising influence when conquest, torture and diplomacy had failed.

Inevitably, the Romans became great connoisseurs of wine—inevitably because the Roman temperament was worldly and sensual. Their immense mental energy tended to spread out sideways, into planning and scheming and conquest, not upwards into ideas and religious speculation. At their best—in the pre-Caesarian period—the Romans displayed the virtues of balance and good sense, strong family feeling, respect for the law, ability to compromise. These virtues enabled them to survive the severe inner conflicts between patricians and plebeians. If the Roman temperament had been more like the Russian, the end result would have been a Russian Revolution, with the slaughter of the patricians; instead, it was a compromise, with the patricians agreeing to hand over much of their power, but still taking an active part in the guiding of the state. And it was after this (287 B.C.) that Rome went on to become really great. And also, unfortunately, extremely rich. 'Rome is a madman's dream', says Shaw's Caesar, as he stares at the sphinx under the night sky, 'This is my reality'. Rome was certainly a madman's dream; its story, as told in Plutarch or Suetonius or Tacitus, is so bloody and stupid and vicious that it sounds like a suburb of Hell. (Those who prefer their history novelised will find a reasonably accurate picture in Grave's Claudius novels—or, for that matter, in the *Satyricon* of Petronius.) But Shaw was indulging in romantic wishful thinking when he made Caesar a poet and a mystic; mysticism, like philosophy, was absent from the Roman temperament.

The Emperor Augustus asked Virgil to write the *Aeneid* to win the Romans back to their primitive virtues; but by then it was too late. Rome was the master of the world and the centre of an empire; luxuries flowed in from every point of the compass. The emperors were casual about committing murder, and were usually murdered themselves—mostly by their own soldiers. After the time of Augustus, being emperor was about as safe as being a Mafia boss in the middle of a gang war. In fact, after the murder of Caracalla in A.D. 217, there was a period of seventy years in which there were seventy-five emperors, an average of one every eleven months.

But at least Roman decadence produced a real interest in wine. To begin with, the Romans imported Greek wines, and may have traded wine with the Etruscans. In the middle of the fourth century B.C., the Romans began to cultivate their own vineyards. By the time of Julius Caesar, the Romans had become the greatest experts on wine in the civilised world. The Greeks and the Persians allowed their vines to grow along the ground, sometimes raising the grapes clear of the dust on short poles. The Romans learned the use of trellises, and tall stakes with horizontal crossbars. This also had the advantage of keeping the grapes clear of mice and foxes. (I had always assumed that the fable of the fox and the grapes was invented by some ignorant townsman; but Varro mentions that foxes were partial to grapes.)

The small Roman farmers of early days made wine to be drunk immediately, or perhaps sold in a tavern or shop attached to the farm. Since most young wine tastes unpleasant, quality would hardly be important. In these early days, most of the trade was conducted by barter. As Rome became rich, it discovered the use of money. Now a man can be very rich in land and cattle, but there is a limited amount he can *do* with his wealth. But a man who is rich in money can buy land or ships or slaves. A rich farmer depends for his wealth on his agricultural skill, but a financier only needs skill in speculation. He can get richer at a pace that leaves the farmer standing, and without doing the slightest good to the community. This new class of rich men began to buy up the small farms of men who had become impoverished fighting for Rome, and they began to cultivate their vineyards with a care that was impossible for a man with a living to make. All this created the bitterness and unrest that eventually destroyed Rome. But in the meantime, Roman vineyards flourished, and Roman wine improved steadily. The volcanic soil around Mount Vesuvius produced some of the best wines. Campania—which includes Vesuvius, as well as Capua and Sorrento—also produced the most highly esteemed Roman wine, Falernian. Labican wine, 'sweet and oily', was kept for at least ten years before being drunk. The Romans knew about racking the wine—drawing off its sediment periodically—and about fining it with the white of pigeons' eggs. (As this sinks slowly to the bottom, it carries fragments of yeast, and other impurities, with it.) As we have seen, the Greeks drank their wine mixed with all kinds of flavouring materials, from honey to seawater, and the Romans frequently did so, especially when on the march. But Columella, a writer on agriculture of the first century A.D., declares that nothing should be added to good wine, either to preserve it or dilute it. (The Romans, like the Greeks, often drank their wine mixed with water.) And with their ten-year-old Falernian or Mamertine wine, the wealthier Romans ate huge meals of highly seasoned fish, poultry and meat—their favourite meat was roast boar. Petronius mentioned dormice dipped in honey and rolled in poppy seed—a great Roman delicacy.

After the great period of wine—from about 130 B.C. to the time of Jesus—there came a century of recession, when there were too many vineyards, and the price sank until it became uneconomical. The Romans overcame this crisis by various expedients; they made their viticulture more scientific and efficient, and the Emperor Domitian passed an edict in A.D. 92 demanding that provincial vineyards (i.e. those of Spain, France, Germany, North Africa) should be reduced by a half. (Fortunately, this was carried out half-heartedly.) The Italians actually began to export wine to the rest of Europe, and Lyons became a great trading centre.

And so the history of wine is closely bound up with the history of Imperial Rome, and with the rise of 'capitalism'. As far as Rome is concerned, capitalism was the basic cause of its downfall—although not for the reasons Karl Marx taught. It destroyed the spirit that made Rome imperialistic; it turned patriotic farmers and freedmen into disgruntled would-be rebels.

But by that time, Roman imperialism had spread the vine from Africa to Germany, and capitalism had brought the making of wine to a high level of perfection. The Romans may not have understood the spirit of Dionysus, but they understood his sacred beverage.

Rome took some five hundred years to die, or rather, to disintegrate; the last emperor—appropriately named Romulus—was deposed in A.D 476. By this time, western history—and western viticulture—was in the hands of the church rather than the state.

It is my own belief—quite unprovable on historical evidence—that there *had* to be a great religious reaction. Mankind was entering a new phase of its evolution, and the old gods were unable to satisfy new needs. The old gods were human in their characteristics: Zeus couldn't resist a pretty figure; Jahweh was bad-tempered and jealous. As to the Romans, they hadn't even enough religious sense to invent their own gods; they borrowed from the Greeks, and their notion of the god-like was so limited that they saw nothing incongruous in raising their emperors to the ranks of the gods. It was a time of great changes; the world had changed more in a few centuries than in the previous three thousand years. There was a huge mass of miserable and oppressed people—another precondition for the appearance of a new religion. Men began to crave for gods who gave them a sense of being quite different from human beings. Christianity was a revolt against Rome; not only against Roman imperialism and capitalism, but against Roman psychological limitations, Roman stupidity. The European spirit was beginning to need a new dimension of spirituality. When Nero persecuted the Christians—because he needed a scapegoat for the burning of Rome—he only made them stronger, for persecution was precisely what was needed to bring this new religion of world-rejection to full consciousness.

The churches and monasteries were not solely responsible for the continuation of viticulture in the Dark Ages. The wines of the Rhône and the Gironde (which we now call claret) were well established on a commercial basis long before the rise of the monasteries, in the sixth and seventh centuries. But it was monks—and nuns—who preserved the tradition of wine growing; they had the time to devote to it.

The Dark Ages of Europe—from the fall of Rome to, say, the Crusades of the twelfth century—are also the dark ages of wine. For how can the vine survive as war floods across the land like the lava from an erupting volcano? This is what happened for almost two centuries. Europe and the Near East were overwhelmed with tides of invaders from the colder regions of the north. A tribe called the Goths originated in Sweden, moved to southern Russia, where they divided into Ostrogoths and Visigoths (Eastern and Western Goths), and began to harass Greece and Rome in the third century A.D. It was largely the pressure of these barbarian invaders that decided Constantine the Great to move his capital from Rome—which was badly placed, halfway down Italy—to Byzantium, in the south of the Black Sea (A.D. 330). This move might have preserved the Roman Empire for centuries longer; but in A.D. 372, a tribe of savage Mongolian horsemen upset the whole balance of power by invading Europe. This tribe was called the Huns; the Great Wall of China had been built to keep them out, but they had conquered China. Now they began to pour westward, and other barbarian tribes were either forced to retreat, or (like the Ostrogoths) to become their subjects. The Vandals, Alans and Sueves poured across Gaul, and in three years (406–409) completely ravaged the land; later, there were waves of Franks and Visigoths. The Visigoths had been allowed to settle in the Roman Empire—in Thrace—but under the leadership of a brilliant general, Alaric, they turned on their hosts, and eventually sacked Rome in A.D. 410. (The Vandals made their name a synonym for wanton destructiveness when they sacked Rome in 455.) The Huns also reached Gaul, and were finally defeated there in 451; but they had played their part in history: to inaugurate the Dark Ages. Rome fell to barbarians from East Germany in 476, the end of the great Roman Empire. Two great barbarian leaders emerged from this melting pot of war and destruction: Theodoric the Goth, who, for a while, looked as if he was going to create his own great Gothic empire with its seat in Italy, and Clovis the Frank. The Franks, originally a small German tribe, invaded Gaul and gave it their name—France. Clovis became a Christian, and the first of a line of kings. His significance for this history is that he stabilised France.

The Germanic invaders learned to speak the Latinised tongue of the natives, which became the French we know today. And because Clovis became a Christian, the churches and monasteries were able to carry on their business peacefully. And an important part of their business was tending their vines, to make Communion wine.

The age of invasions was still not over. In the century after the death of the prophet Mahomet (632), the Arabs surged across Europe and the Near East; they took Spain from the Visigoths, besieged Constantinople (without success) and even reached the Chinese border. They were finally defeated near Poitiers by Charles Martel (732); otherwise, it is possible that the whole of Europe, including England, might have been Moslemised and had teetotalism thrust upon it. This Charles Martel was not a king, but only a general; technically speaking, he was a servant of the descendants of King Clovis. But this line of kings (known as Merovingians) had become enfeebled, and Charles Martel's son, Pepin, became the first king of a new line, the Carolingians. And Pepin's son, Charlemagne, became one of the greatest emperors Europe had seen since Constantine. This meant that France could once again continue with the business of making wine undisturbed by major catastrophes.

All these words about invasions and battles falsify the truth of history: what really went on when an army invaded a foreign country and pillaged it. I have commented elsewhere* on the behaviour of the first waves of Crusaders who set out in the twelfth century to avenge Christendom for the fall of Jerusalem; as soon as they got into countries with a foreign language they proceeded to rape and loot; another army that reached Constantinople committed such outrages that the Emperor Alexius hastened to ship them across the Bosphorus to Turkey, where they were promptly cut to pieces by the Turks. In those barbaric ages, an invader felt himself free to do what he liked the moment he found himself in a foreign country; he gave way to every violent urge; if he had always wondered what it would be like to cut open the belly of a pregnant woman, or toss a baby in the air and try to cut it in two with his sword, now was his chance to find out. When a village had been looted and its

* *A Casebook of Murder*, Chapter 1.

women raped, it seemed the most natural thing in the world to set it on fire, for all human beings enjoy watching a fire. This should be remembered when we read some statistic about war—such as that the Vandals, Alans and Sueves spent three years raiding Gaul. Three years of slaughter would leave the natives with little heart for replanting their orchards and pruning their vines. It is no wonder we know absolutely nothing about the history of wine in the Dark Ages.

William Younger has one of those passages that breathe life into the facts of history.* After commenting that the Middle Ages were an age of total inefficiency, 'grossly and contentedly incompetent', he goes on:

'Darkness and cold were commonplace. Where the poor had lighting at all, it was rudimentary, and heating, even in the great houses, was scarcely more advanced. . . . Some chimneys existed in England in manor-houses or castles or monasteries, but many an upper class Englishman lit his fire against a screen in the "hall" where he ate. . . . A draught of wine must often have warmed a chilled courtier, stamping his feet on a fireless evening; and one shivers in sympathy with the Rhenish peasants in those two terrible winters of 1125 and 1126 when men and cattle were frozen to death and birds fell dead out of the sky.'

The *Weinchronik* of Deichmann and Wolf records that in the ninth century, thirty out of thirty-seven vintages were small or bad, and in the eleventh century, twenty-nine out of thirty-seven were bad. The freezing cold of the winters was varied by summers that were so hot that rivers dried up and over a thousand men and animals died of heat in one area alone. In some years, peasants in wine-growing areas starved because the vintages were so poor; in other years they starved because the vintage was so abundant that there was enormous over-production. Younger mentions one place in Franconia where there was so much wine that it was mixed with lime for building.

Wine was also a welcome alternative to water, which was frequently polluted. It must be borne in mind that the world knew nothing about germs until the mid-nineteenth century (as late as 1849, Semmelweis was dismissed from a hospital for insisting that doctors ought to wash their hands before delivering

* *Gods, Men and Wine*, p. 253.

babies). In the Middle Ages, the only objection to sewage getting into the water supply was that it spoiled the taste. Younger mentions a village in the Pyrenees where he was shown a pool that contained 'the finest drinking water in the valley'—and which was a couple of hundred yards below the point where the sewage flowed into the stream. I myself recently spent a winter in the Majorcan village of Deya, and became thoroughly familiar with the smell of the garbage dumped into the dry bed of the local stream throughout the summer; it stayed there until the winter rains produced a torrent that washed it out to sea. For the first week, the whole family suffered from stomach pains and diarrhoea which, we were assured, was perfectly normal for newcomers. . . . *

All this makes it possible to understand why wine was more than a mere beverage in the Middle Ages. It became a symbol of life and happiness: not only because it produced lightness of heart, but because people who drank it habitually—such as monks—were likelier to be healthier and live longer than those who drank only water. No wonder the fat, jolly cleric was one of the stock figures of the Middle Ages. In England, it was ale that was drunk in monasteries; for although the English had vines, there is no evidence that wine-making ever caught on. Giraldus Cambrensis, a travel writer of the twelfth century, describes the feasting and general good-living he found at Canterbury. G. G. Coulton says of Canterbury—and its rival, the Abbey of Westminster—'Of bread and ale there are different qualities, and the brethren in each case are to have the finest. Here, as in all other cases where similar records have survived, the lowest allowance of ale is a gallon each per diem'. That is to say, most of the monks had literally 'one over the eight' every day of their lives.

Because the Middle Ages had lost the Roman skill in viticulture, much of its wine was nasty and vinegary. People drank it to get drunk, not for the taste, which must have been bad enough to scour the throat. All wine was drunk in the year it was made—as Beaujolais is nowadays; but much of it was even drunk before it was racked—i.e. before the impurities had time to sink to the bottom. 'Racked wine' (or wine of rec) was

* When I left there was talk of instituting a system of garbage collection.

regarded as something of a luxury. The Romans knew how to stop the wine from turning sour in the barrel by pouring a layer of olive oil on top of it, so the air could not get at it. The vintners of the Middle Ages found this refinement unnecessary, since the wine was drunk so quickly. The consequence was that much of the wine was half vinegar by the time it reached the customer. Even so, there were poor countries where this sour wine—which we might use for cooking—could be profitably sold or bartered. Younger mentions a licence, dated 1401, for a shipper to take 30 tuns of undrinkable wine to Ireland and trade it for salmon. He also mentions that wine merchants were unwilling to waste vinegary wine, and mixed it with new wine for sale in taverns. One taverner, convicted in 1346 of selling such a wine, was sentenced to lose his licence, and also to drink a draught of his own liquor and have the rest poured over his head.

Wine came to England with the Norman conquest, and thereafter was generally available. Younger gives some fascinating paragraphs of prices: shortly after the conquest, wine was a penny a gallon, and a day labourer's wages were twopence a day. Oysters cost a ha'penny a hundred and a salmon one shilling. In 1368, a sword cost two shillings, and wine had gone up to sixpence a gallon.

The reason the wine trade continued to flourish so long after the Norman conquest—and, presumably, after most Normans had become thoroughly anglicised—was that Henry II of England married Eleanor of Aquitaine, and acquired Aquitaine, Gascony, and various other excellent wine-producing regions of western France, the land of Bordeaux. From then on, the fortunate English could drink French wine as easily as their home-brewed beer—another good reason for not attempting to make English wine.

We may say that the Middle Ages ended when Columbus discovered America, in the last decade of the fifteenth century. It also happens to be one of those periods, like the fifth century in Greece, when there was a sudden flowering of human genius—Michelangelo, Leonardo, Dürer, Copernicus, Cornelius Agrippa, Paracelsus, Rabelais. Europe, like the civilisation of the Greeks and the Romans, had passed through its harsh period; a gentler and more civilised age began; the word 'renaissance' is appropriate. Once again, wine was appreciated for other qualities than its power to induce drunkenness, and an awareness of the finer points of gastronomy began to develop.

The English were fortunately placed; although they grew no vines of their own, they had a good navy, and all the wine of Europe was at their disposal. The Rhine flows into the sea in Holland, and the Rhenish wine also flowed up this waterway and across to England. The wine of Gascony continued to be enormously popular. England had also formed strong trading links with Spain and Portugal. And it was from Jerez, in southern Spain, that the wine called 'sack'—and later sherry—came to Elizabethan England. The Elizabethans were fond of their sack, as we gather from Shakespeare. The word 'sack' may be derived from *sec*—dry—or from the fact that the grape juice was strained through sacking. Our modern sherry is a fortified wine—that is to say, its alcoholic strength is increased by the addition of grape brandy.* Falstaff's sack was probably the straight wine.

The peculiarity of modern sherry—apart from the addition of brandy—is that the barrel in which it is matured is not kept refilled with wine; as the wine evaporates, an air gap is created, which would cause most wines to oxidise; but in Andalusia (the 'Baetica' of the Romans, a good wine-growing area even then), a yeast called 'flor' forms on top of the wine and protects it from acetic acid bacteria. This flor—which looks like flakes of chalk—consumes all the sugar—so that all natural sherries are dry—and leaves the peculiar sherry taste. (The sweetness in sweet sherry is added later.) The wine is then carefully blended—small quantities of older wine being added to the younger year by year, until the right blend is achieved. We do not know whether Falstaff drank a wine made in this way, or whether he simply drank a wine made like any other wine in Jerez. There must have been some peculiar and captivating quality about sack, apart from its power to warm the blood and make the face glow (which Falstaff describes): perhaps simply the fact that it

* A puzzling classification, which means simply any brandy that is not a Cognac or Armagnac. It is called grape brandy to distinguish it from cherry brandy, apricot brandy, etc.

is more fragrant than most wines. On the other hand, he mulled it, and probably dropped herbs and spices into it; so perhaps, after all, it was only its cheapness that recommended it.

When I was writing a novel called *The Philosopher's Stone*, I went to some trouble to find out exactly what it would be like if some time machine could take us back to the London of Shakespeare's day; it was an interesting exercise in reconstruction. This is a part of it:

'I was in a narrow, winding street, with timbered houses that almost met overhead. The stink came from the cobbles underfoot, which were slippery with excrement, urine and fragments of food. A broad open sewer ran down the middle of the street. But the people walking along the street did not seem to be bothered by the smell. . . . Enormous blow-flies buzzed over the sewer. . . . A coach with two horses was actually clattering along the street, its wheels on either side of the sewer. It had no springs, and jarred and bumped on the cobbles. Most of the people looked extremely poor. A fairly well-dressed man who came out of a yard between the houses was wearing metal objects strapped to his feet, which lifted him three or four inches above the sewage; he walked clumsily, with a clanking noise. . . .

'On all four corners of the street, there were vendors selling cooked food from carts. The one nearest to me was selling cooked fish from a large earthenware bowl. On a wooden slab beside this there was cabbage—the leaves cooked as they lay on top of one another, so they formed a kind of block; the vendor simply sliced parts off this block as though it were cheese. The lumps of fish and mussels floating in the earthenware bowl looked curiously unappetising.'

The narrator also mentions rats strolling along the street as casually as cats. A girl of sixteen who looks pretty from behind turns round and proves to have the left nostril missing, as if cut off by a knife, and the number of disfigured people is generally much larger than in modern London; large numbers of women, even young ones, had hair streaked with grey, due to vitamin deficiency. There are also many obese men and women—grossly, wobblingly fat.

The kind of tavern to which Shakespeare and Ben Jonson might resort would be rather like certain old inns that still exist in remote parts of the British Isles. It might have floorboards, or the floor might be made of earth packed tight; in either case, it would probably be covered with straw, for Elizabethan drinkers regarded the floor as the natural place to spit upon. The wine and ale would be in barrels on a low rack or counter; there were still no corks, so wine was seldom kept in bottles. Shakespeare would have asked for a bottle of sack, and his quart bottle would have been filled from the barrel and cost fourpence (although at Oxford, according to Edmund Penning-Rowsell, it cost two shillings a gallon in 1580). It might be a more or less globular object with a flat base and a short neck with a handle attached —probably made of pot—or it might be an odd-shaped bottle of thick green glass. Our present tendency to have tall, thin bottles would have struck the Elizabethans as rather absurd; after all, the taller a bottle, the easier it is to knock it over; their bottles tended to be squat, with more width than height; in the three or four centuries since then, bottles have slowly become narrower and taller. Shakespeare would have taken his bottle over to a plain wooden table, sat on a plain wooden bench, and lit up his pipe—smoking in taverns became popular in the second half of Elizabeth's reign. He could have ordered food, but might well have contented himself by chewing radishes dipped in salt.

The Elizabethans had reason to be fond of their taverns, for it was against the law to keep wine at home—except for lords. Sir Walter Raleigh managed to get the right to grant tavern licences, and there is evidence to show that he took advantage of it to line his own pocket. Another of the disillusioning things about the close study of history is that some of our great national heroes, like Raleigh and Drake, turn out on closer examination to have been little more than rascally adventurers. On the other hand, perhaps we should expect this. We feel surprise because we think the Elizabethans should have been as basically respectable and law-abiding as we are. The truth is, the ferment and confusion of Elizabethan England was much like the ferment and confusion of California during the gold rush, or New York in the 1890s, or even Chicago in the 1920s; it would have been unusual for a man of character not to be a bit of a rogue. In spite of this law forbidding the keeping of wine in most households, the Elizabethans had a considerable degree of freedom in their drinking habits. If wine cost a great deal more than the penny a gallon it had cost under William the Conqueror, this was not because the Queen taxed it heavily; the French themselves taxed all wine not carried to England by French ships; and since it was still cheaper to pay the tax and use an English ship than to hire a French ship, the cost was passed on to the consumer.

Most of the historians of wine have harsh things to say about James I. Being a grasping man, and less concerned than Elizabeth with popularity with the British taxpayer, he took a larger percentage from the cost of wine—which forced up the price—and allowed various abuses where licensing was concerned. The Elizabethan law against keeping wine in an ordinary household may sound an incursion on natural freedom; in fact, it kept wine in the taverns, and kept the price stable. As soon as anybody could purchase a licence, and private individuals could also purchase the right to collect duty on wine (butlerage), the whole field was open to speculators; the price shot up, and wine soon became too expensive for the working man.

Most working men took to beer. But there was an alternative: spirits. The very name—spirits—reveals its origin: the spirit, or essence, of wine or beer or any other fermented liquor. The alchemists, in their search for the essence of natural substances, discovered brandy—probably as early as the thirteenth century. But although it was no doubt appreciated in the depths of the countryside in midwinter, it never replaced wine or beer as a popular, everyday beverage. In England, the avarice of James I changed all that. The laws about wine did not apply to spirits; anyone could ferment a mixture of apples, plums, sour wine and beer dregs, distil the resulting gutrot, and keep any quantity of this throat-burning aqua vitae on his premises, or sell it in the street. (In Shakespeare's day, it was not sold in taverns.) It did not take long for someone to discover that a cornmash made a better quality schnapps. Early in the seventeenth century, a Dutchman named Franciscus de la Boe (also known as Dr Sylvius) discovered that a strong and cheap spirit could be made from rye flavoured with juniper berries; it was called 'geneva' (juniper), shortened to gin. In Ireland, the peasants made a mash of barley malt, and distilled the resulting beer to make a spirit which they called 'usquebaugh'. The word was later anglicised to whiskey.

Gin came to England with William of Orange in 1689, as claret had come with William the Conqueror. Naturally, Dutch Billy preferred the English to drink Dutch gin to French brandy, and made sure that it was cheaper.

I have described the result in *A Casebook of Murder;* for the introduction of this cheap drink caused a sudden and very steep rise in the crime rate. This is understandable. Shakespeare and Ben Jonson could get pleasantly tipsy on their fourpenny quart of Rhenish or claret or sack; but in the London of William and Mary, tuppence would buy a pint of gin, justifying the notice displayed in many taverns 'Drunk for a penny, dead drunk for tuppence'. The effect on a population that had been accustomed to beer, cider and sack was similar to the effect of hard drugs in London or New York: that is, people enjoyed the sensation so much that they robbed or committed assault to get the necessary twopence. The result was that in 1699, only ten years after William came to the throne, it was thought necessary to pass a law making the theft of goods worth more than five shillings a hanging matter. The majority of shoplifters were women and children, so the execution of women and children became commonplace. London, which had been a reasonably safe city in the days of Queen Elizabeth, became a sink of crime.

Hogarth dramatised the problem in his two etchings of Beer Street and Gin Lane. In Beer Street, men are pleasantly engaged in debate, relaxed and cheerful as they drink; in Gin Lane, a mother allows her baby to fall out of her arms into a court below; a madman has impaled a child on a stake; a man has hanged himself in an attic; workmen pledge their tools at the pawnbroker. It sounds like one of those pathetic Victorian ballads:

Poor Mary has no mother
Her mother she is dead.
Her father is a drunkard
And will not buy her bread.

But there was justification for Hogarth's picture. The *Newgate Calendar* records the case of Judith Dufour, who collected her baby from a workhouse, where it had been dressed in new clothes; she strangled the baby and threw its body in a ditch, then sold the clothes for one shilling and fourpence, which she spent on gin. The *Newgate Calendar* and *Lives of Remarkable Criminals* testify to the steady rise in crimes of this sort—pointless, sickening and pathetic.

In the forty years that followed William's accession, gin production had risen from half a million gallons a year to three and a half million. (I am indebted to Alec Waugh for the figures.) A 'Gin Act' of 1736 which attempted to put a brake on the sale of gin was completely unsuccessful, and by 1744 the yearly consumption was nineteen million gallons. The poor felt they had a right to escape from their misery. It is worth bearing in mind that the total population of England at that time was about ten million (although figures are unreliable), and that gin drinking was confined to the poor in big cities; the 'average gin drinker' got through half a gallon to a gallon a week. (This leaves out of account the consumption of other distilled spirits—brandy, schnapps and so on.)

The middle and upper classes stuck to beer and wine—claret and port were the favourite wines. Younger has some interesting figures. James Boswell's uncle drank five bottles of claret a day, and John Mytton, a drunken sportsman, drank six bottles of port a day, starting at breakfast. Goethe, whom no one ever accused of alcoholism, drank two litres of wine a day even when taking a cure at Carlsbad. Dr Johnson said that the good citizens of Lichfield were drunk every evening of the week, and no one thought any the worse of them for it. The country squire usually staggered off to bed when he could no longer stand up or keep awake. The gentry in towns became increasingly fond of punch, or 'negus' (invented by Colonel Francis Negus)— a drink with a wine or spirit base, and flavoured with nutmeg, honey, sugar, oranges, lemons, or any other chopped fruit that happened to be available; it was often diluted with water, which, in winter, was usually hot. Punch satisfied all the necessities for a party drink: it had a pleasant taste, was reasonably cheap, and produced an agreeable intoxication. It became immensely popular; the punchbowl was to be found in every sideboard in England; it became as much a part of English life as the mixing bowl became in Greece or Rome.

The Age of Elegance was also an age of drunkenness. Perhaps it spread upward from the poorer classes; or perhaps it was due to the increased prosperity of the middle classes. Whatever the reason, it began to disappear towards the end of the century—and this applies to Europe as well as to England. One reason may be surmised from De Quincey's *Confessions of an English Opium Eater*: laudanum, a mixture of opium and alcohol, could be bought at any chemist's shop for a few pence, and people with serious psychological problems often became laudanum addicts rather than alcoholics. (According to De Quincey, laudanum had definite advantages over alcohol; the sense of exaltation and detachment it produced was calmer, and lasted longer.) Or perhaps the factories and 'dark satanic mills' offered the poor a better chance of making a living, so that gin ceased to be the only escape from misery and despair. Younger even suggests that the decline in drunkenness was due to the increased popularity of tea, although this strikes me as the least plausible of hypotheses.

In one sense, the eighteenth century was the most important epoch in the history of wine since the great days of Roman viticulture. There are two reasons: Europe had discovered the cork and the cylindrical bottle.

Now cork *was* known to the ancient world as a stopper. But it was of no particular use with wide-necked amphoras. As we have already seen, when the Greeks or Romans wanted to age their wines, they used a mixture of clay, wax, leaves (or fabric) and string. Cork was rediscovered in Europe sometime before the age of Shakespeare—we know that because Shakespeare has a reference to it—but was not made use of by the Elizabethans because they preferred to drink their wines young.

In the late seventeenth century, a monk of Champagne named Dom Perignon discovered that if wine is sealed up in a bottle while it is still fermenting—or refermenting, as it tends to in spring—the result is a sparkling wine,* which became known as

* The Italians knew sparkling wine earlier, but it was cloudy and muddy.

saute bouchon, cork popper. The trouble is that such '*vin diable*' often broke the bottle. But the quality was found to be so refreshing that the wine growers set out to solve this problem by strengthening the bottles and inserting expanding corks. It was a difficult problem, for the glass might have a fault invisible to the naked eye; consequently, the maker of champagne expected to lose between a quarter and a half of his stock. It was not until the eighteenth century that breakages became rare.

If champagne could be sold in bottles, why not other wines? Again, there were problems. The cork tended to shrink, and let in air, which ruined the wine. Someone discovered that if the wine bottle was kept on its side, so the cork remained moist, no shrinkage occurred; but the clumsy, often mis-shapen bottles of the Elizabethans were unsuitable for storing in racks. However, the art of glass-blowing improved in the eighteenth century, and bottles were made 'long' and cylindrical instead of short and more-or-less round. Of course, it had always been known that wines improve with age. Some wines may be almost undrinkable when young, owing to the tannin content (tannin being a constituent of the stalks, skins and pips of the grape)—the Turks make a heavily-tanninised wine called Bogazker, 'the strangler' —but they age superbly. It was during the early eighteenth century that wine growers—and the noblemen who could afford to lay down a cellar—discovered that when these heavy wines are kept in a tightly-corked bottle, they continue to mature until all the harshness has vanished; the resulting wine may have a subtlety and beauty of flavour that could never have been suspected in its earlier years. With amazement, the wine growers realised that they had been wasting their best wines, blending them with other wines to make them less harsh. Kept for a few years, they could turn into a kind of nectar—and also, incidentally, increase their value tenfold. The age of connoisseurship had finally arrived.

This is not the end of the history of wine, but the rest can be conveniently told in the course of discussing the wines themselves.

TWO

France: The World's Vineyard

IT IS A STRANGE thought that although man has been drinking beer and wine for thousands of years, it was only about a century ago that he discovered exactly *why* sweet grape juice turns into sour-tasting wine. The man who made the discovery was a short-sighted little Frenchman named Louis Pasteur. As a young man, he became a professor in Lille; one day in 1856, he was approached by an alcohol distiller named Bigo, who was concerned that some of his vats of fermenting sugar-beet were 'sick', and failing to produce alcohol. Pasteur took samples of the 'sick' ferment and of healthy ferment from other vats. He looked at the healthy ferment under his microscope, and saw that the grains of yeast were sprouting tiny buds; clearly, this yeast was a living thing. He looked at the sick ferment, and saw there was no yeast—only very small rod-like creatures, tinier than the yeast, wriggling around. The smell of the sick ferment led him to examine sour milk, and there he found the same rod-like creatures. It dawned on him that organic processes like the making of cheese, alcohol and yoghourt are due to the activity of these tiny animals. The famous German chemist Liebig contradicted Pasteur: he said that albumen was the real producer of the alcohol. It was hard to prove him wrong, for yeast refused to multiply in a mixture without albumen—until Pasteur one day discovered accidentally that ammonia would serve just as well. Into a test tube he introduced a mixture of distilled water, ammonia, sugar and yeast; the yeast sprouted and multiplied, and in no time at all—alcohol. Liebig was refuted.*

* As to M. Bigo and his problem, Pasteur's discovery apparently led to the solution. M. Bigo's son wrote somewhat obscurely: 'Pasteur had noticed through the microscope that the globules were round when fermentation was healthy, that they lengthened when alteration began, and were quite long when fermentation became lactic. This very simple method allowed us to watch the process and avoid the failures in fermentation. . . .' *Life of Pasteur* by R. Vallery-Radot.

The process that takes its name from Pasteur—pasteurisation—was devised to improve wine, not milk. The wine growers of Artois—Pasteur's home town—asked him to investigate various 'sicknesses' of their wines: some tasted bitter, some sour, some as if old sacks had been steeped in it. Pasteur looked at the wines under his microscope and found viruses for each of these sicknesses. He discovered that they could be cured by heating the wine slightly after it had finished fermenting—but not enough to spoil it.

It was also Pasteur who demonstrated conclusively that the yeast that makes the wine is on the skins of the grapes. He boiled grape juice, to kill the yeast, and kept it in a sealed flask for weeks; there was no fermentation. He washed some newly plucked grapes, and introduced a drop of the water into his flask of sterile grape juice; fermentation started almost immediately. . . .

Burgundy

The monks who tended the vineyards of Burgundy and Bordeaux knew nothing about the varieties of yeast that produce different types of wine. All they knew was that if the vines are carefully pruned and tended, and the wine made with loving care, the result was a good wine. And if they became careless and casual, the wine also became coarse. It was almost as if the wine thrived on love and attention, like a baby.

As we have already observed, it was to the monasteries that France owes her eminence as a wine producer. Even if England had been able to grow grapes—which is possible—it is doubtful if we could have learned to produce great wines after the dissolution of the monasteries. And the French Revolution almost produced a similar catastrophe in Burgundy. The big estates were broken up and sold piecemeal; a once famous vineyard might end up packaged between four owners, each in charge of a piece the size of a small garden. This is why there is such bewildering variety in the wine of Burgundy. Bordeaux, being further from the centre of disturbance—Paris—managed to survive without similar upheavals. And that, according to some wine experts, explains why you can drink a fine claret almost every week of the year, while you may be lucky to encounter an exceptional burgundy even once a year. This is a matter on which I am not prepared to venture an opinion, except to remark that the real pity is that Burgundy was just learning to produce great wine when the Revolution came. In the seventeenth century, its wines were rough and harsh. The invention of the corked bottle brought a new care to wine making; burgundy had just reached its natural position as the greatest wine in the world when the Revolution set it back fifty years. For it is obvious that if an excellent vineyard is divided between several owners, some will be less conscientious than others; yet every one of these owners has the right to call his wine by the name of the vineyard. The resulting confusion did no good to the reputation of Burgundy.

This country of Burgundy, which takes its name from a German tribe, the Burgundii (who invaded around the year A.D. 500) stretches between Dijon and Lyon. Its main part, from Dijon to Santenay, is known as the Golden Slope, the Côte d'Or. These slopes are the hills that surround the course of the river Saône—although most of the great wine-producing country of the Golden Slope lies some kilometres to the west of the river. It is only in the south, the country of the lesser wines, Mâcon and Beaujolais, that the vineyards follow the actual course of the river valley.

All the great wines of Burgundy are made from the Pinot grape, the aristocrat of the grape family. In Roman days, the Pinot grape was the sole occupant of the French vineyards. Then some Crusader discovered that a Near Eastern grape, the Gamay, produces half as much juice again as the Pinot, and vintners who were more interested in quantity than quality began to plant the Gamay. It is only in Beaujolais that the Gamay produces a wholly satisfactory wine. Even so, it is a wine to be drunk like beer, not sipped. Mâcon wines, like Beaujolais, are light and easy to drink, although they tend to be coarser than a good Beaujolais; they may be made of a blend of Pinot and Gamay.

The first thing I taught my children about wine—when they reached the age of about four—was to distinguish between claret and burgundy by the bottle; burgundy is in the bottle with the sloping shoulders, claret in the narrower bottle with round shoulders. Authorities say the burgundy bottle is more 'authentic', historically speaking; it certainly *looks* the kind of bottle that would hold the king of wines.

In fact, all bottles with sloping shoulders do not contain burgundy. South of Lyon, the wine-growing area continues down the valley of the Rhône to Avignon; these wines are called Rhône rather than burgundy; the best known of them in England is Châteauneuf du Pape, which the English tend to find too heavy to drink in quantity.

It is almost as easy to distinguish a burgundy (or Rhône) from a claret by the taste as by the bottle, although this is difficult to put into words. When I began drinking wine regularly, in 1956, I did not care for claret, and if asked what I disliked about it, I would have said it was *too* dry, too 'thin', sometimes too acid. A good burgundy or Rhône goes admirably with a chunk of cheese and an onion; it has a robust, muscular quality, the kind of thing that tempts wine writers to get fanciful and start talking about the Three Musketeers. In *Lear*, Shakespeare refers to 'waterish Burgundy'—which is just about the last adjective that anyone would associate with that wine.

As to myself, I was converted to claret sometime in 1957, when someone bought me an exceptionally good bottle with my dinner in a Soho restaurant. A real wine writer would take care to tell you the name and year of the wine, and even the name of the restaurant, but I am afraid I've forgotten all three. It was certainly not one of the great five—Lafite, Margaux, Latour, Haut-Brion or Mouton-Rothschild; probably just an ordinary Pomerol, from my memory of its taste and colour. Pomerol might, without too much inaccuracy, be compared to Beaujolais; it is lighter than many clarets, matures quicker, has a deeper colour and more flavour, and is gentle on the palate. I realised then the peculiar advantages of a good claret, the lightness and the velvety texture.

A couple of months ago, I spent a day driving around Cornwall with Michael Harrison, the novelist and historian of Victorian London; we had drunk a couple of pints of beer with lunch, and done some strenuous sightseeing; at half-past five in the evening, we walked into my local pub, and I ordered sandwiches and a bottle of wine. I asked him whether he would prefer burgundy or Bordeaux. 'Oh, Bordeaux, definitely. I don't feel up to burgundy.' What he implied—and what most wine authorities would strenuously deny—is that claret is somehow a lighter wine than burgundy, perhaps even less intoxicating. But after drinking at midday, I knew exactly what he meant. There is definitely a sense in which claret seems lighter and more harmless than burgundy.

Saintsbury has a story about burgundy, which illustrates a point. He tells of an old aunt whose oculist recommended her to drink burgundy, reasoning, presumably, that even if it did not improve her sight, it would reconcile her to its defectiveness. The aunt asked Saintsbury's advice, and he gave her a private winetasting, beginning with an expensive Richebourg, and also introducing her to a 'sound but inexpensive' Pommard. The aunt's income was not large; nevertheless, she said, 'I think, my dear boy, that the best always *is* the best', and ordered a small supply of the Richebourg. Saintsbury evidently feels that this story is rather to his aunt's credit, that she knew a good wine when she tasted one. My own feeling is that it illustrates the wine snobbery of the inexperienced drinker. Richebourg is, of course, one of the great names in Burgundy, the vineyard being a mere nineteen acres near the town of Vosne-Romanée; and if burgundy can be compared to the Three Musketeers, then this one is Porthos—big, with a deep voice. I personally find it a little too 'sturdy'. Pommard, on the other hand, is one of the least heavy wines of the Golden Slope; although immensely popular, and produced in large quantities (probably far more wine than ever grew in the Pommard district), it has its own character and individuality. Purely as a matter of enjoyment, Saintsbury's aunt would almost certainly have found Pommard the better buy—especially since, at that date (second half of the nineteenth century), it would certainly have been genuine Pommard. (If Saintsbury had really wanted to be tactful and helpful, he would have persuaded his aunt to try the *vin rosé* of Marsannay, the northernmost village of the Golden Slope; for this certainly qualifies as a burgundy, and its lightness and freshness would have been more agreeable to an old lady's palate.)

The simplest way to discuss the wines of Burgundy is to take them in geographical order, starting in the north and moving south.

Most of its great wines are produced in a narrow strip known as the Côte de Nuits (after its most famous town, Nuits-St-Georges), which begins some ten kilometres south of Dijon, and extends south for a mere twenty kilometres. Most of its wines are characterised by a certain 'weight', the kind of thing you notice instantly if you buy any bottle labelled 'Nuits-St-Georges'. Marsannay, already mentioned, is not generally recognised as belonging to this distinguished area (which is, no doubt, because several of these vineyards near Dijon are planted with the Gamay as well as the Pinot grape), although it stakes its claim by calling itself Marsannay-la-Côte. (It produces a pleasant but undistinguished red wine as well as the excellent rosé.) The same applies to Fixin, a few kilometres further south. Its wine resembles that of its neighbour, Gevrey-Chambertin.

At this point, I must break off to explain the significance of these double-barrelled names. The explanation is not particularly creditable to the French wine trade. The greatest vineyard of the area is Chambertin, a mere thirty-two acres that produces one of the world's finest wines. Now Gevrey is a town eight miles south of Dijon, with hundreds of acres of vineyards, including Chambertin. To the uninitiated, Gevrey-Chambertin sounds as if it means a Chambertin from Gevrey, as if Chambertin was the commune, and Gevrey was one of its vineyards. This is rather as if every English beer decided to add 'Guinness' to its name, for the sake of the free advertisement. In a strict sense, the commune wine of Gevrey has no right to add Chambertin to its name, for Gevrey-Chambertin is just a good, ordinary, heavy red wine, without a trace of the nobility of real Chambertin. And Chambolle-Musigny, another wine of the Côte de Nuits, has no real right to imply that it is somehow connected with the wine of Les Musigny, another of the great wines. Chambolle-Musigny is not to be sneered at; it is a very pleasant burgundy, rather lighter in body than most—I drank a bottle a day for years until recently. (Then the quality seemed to deteriorate; the wine, when newly opened, had a faint smell which could be compared to stinging nettles or cat piss; after being left open a few hours, this vanished, but the wine then seemed to lack its old lightness.) But it is not to be compared to the superb, delicate wines of Les Musigny, with their bouquet that has been compared to violets or raspberries.

The case of Charmes-Chambertin, is slightly different; this is a vineyard adjoining Chambertin, and of about the same size; its wines are gentler and more distinguished than Gevrey-Chambertin, but not of the same quality as Chambertin itself. Since the two vineyards are separated only by a narrow track, this is an interesting example of the way that two completely different wines can be produced from the same soil and the same grapes, with only a few yards between them. No one is quite certain why this is so—although when one slope faces east and the other west, the reason is obvious enough; otherwise, it remains one of the strange mysteries of viniculture.*

Let us continue with our survey of the wines of Burgundy, travelling south. Between the area of Gevrey-Chambertin and that of Chambolle-Musigny, there lies one of the least known of the wine areas of the Golden Slope, Morey-St-Denis. Once again, St-Denis is the name of its most famous vineyard, which produces one of the *Grand Cru* (great growth) wines (although lighter in quality than most of the great burgundies). The commune wine labelled Morey-St-Denis is somewhere midway between the strength of Gevrey-Chambertin and the lighter elegance of Chambolle-Musigny; if you see it on a restaurant wine list, I strongly recommend you to try it, for it deserves to be as well known as its two neighbours. Its *grands crus*, apart from St-Denis, are Bonnes Mares, Clos de la Roche and the oddly named Clos de Tart, whose name must have explained why the Victorians did not rate it highly.

Chambolle-Musigny I have already mentioned, one of the lighter and more delicate burgundies, when it is in good form. Apart from Les Musigny, its 'great' vineyard is Bonnes Mares, which it shares with Morey, and its delicacy is closer to the Musigny wines than to those of Morey. Next on this southern

* The word 'viniculture' refers to the growing of the wine grape; viticulture refers to grapes in general. In this volume, I have preferred to use viticulture for grape-growing, and to speak of the growing of wine grapes as wine-growing.

route are three names known to wine-lovers all over the world: Vougeot, Vosne-Romanée and Nuits-St-Georges. The vines of Vougeot were planted by monks from the Benedictine Abbey of Cluny, near Mâcon; these monks disliked the luxurious life at Cluny, and took themselves off to a swampy area near Beaune; there they began to produce the superb Vougeot wine. The great wine of the area is Clos de Vougeot (a *clos* is a walled vineyard); the monks lost their vineyard after the Revolution.

Vosne-Romanée is a mere pocket handkerchief in size—only sixty-five acres—but produces some of the most highly prized wines in the world. A list of its wines reads like a kind of Debrett of the wine world: Romanée-Conti, which many would consider to be the world's single greatest wine (a mere four and a half acres!), Richebourg, La Tâche, La Romanée, Romanée Saint-Vivant, and so on. Maurice Healy almost strains his voice as he tries to reach the right note of enthusiasm about La Tâche and Richebourg. This is what he says of a 1904 La Tâche he drank in a Paris restaurant: 'So marvellous, so delicate was the bouquet, it seemed an impertinence to go further and taste the miraculous liquid; and yet, on the palate, it almost made one regret as a waste of time the moments spent in taking the perfume.' This strikes me as Shakespearean in the worst sense of the word—that is, overstrained and rather artificial; yet anyone who has tried to write about wine encounters that basic problem of the inadequacy of language; with so many tastes and aromas and bouquets, one feels the need for a whole battery of new words. It is a pity Wittgenstein drank water; he would have had even more to say about the inadequacy of language if he had tried writing about wine.

And when Healy tries to describe a Richebourg he drank in a London club—a 1923 vintage—he bursts into exclamation marks, 'It was Glorious! Glorious! Glorious!'

The name Romanée-Conti will cause a shadow to pass over the face of those who know their wine history, for it is associated with a tragedy of the vine world. And thereby hangs an interesting story. When colonists from Europe settled the eastern states of America, they tried to make wine from the native grapevines, but found it horrible. It had a foxy taste—which I would describe as being rather like the smell that comes from one of those machines that boils tar and sprays it on roads; it is indescribable, but if you have ever passed such a machine, you know what I mean: not the tarry smell, but the smell that seems to come from the outside of the boiler. The settlers tried planting their own European vines, but found that they were promptly destroyed by some strange disease. It was not until the nineteenth century that it was identified as a tiny bug, the *phylloxera vastatrix*, which attacks the roots of vines. The American vine had developed partial immunity to this pest. They tried crossing American and European vines, and for a while the experiment seemed successful; then the foxy flavour came back. (One of these grapes is called the *Vitis labrusca*, the fox grape.)

Sometime in the 1860s, one of these American vines was brought to Kew Gardens in London. Unfortunately, it contained the phylloxera louse. It was the second great plague sent by the New World to the Old: the first had been syphilis, which Columbus's sailors had caught off the lovely dark-skinned girls of Haiti and Cuba, and which spread across Europe from the brothels of Seville and Barcelona. No one knows how phylloxera spread from Kew Gardens to France; but it did, and in the 1870s, the great vineyards were devastated by it. The European vine had no resistance; the phylloxera spread like the Black Death. For a while, the French believed that their wine industry was at an end. Then someone recalled that the American vines had a natural resistance. They were brought to France, and grafted on to the French vines. It worked. Once again, the French vineyards flourished. But there were certain disadvantages. Admittedly, careful grafting got rid of the disagreeable taste. But American wines had a life of only about twenty-five years, compared to the fifty of European wines. European wines before phylloxera tended to be very long-lived; it is nothing to read in George Saintsbury about an eighty-year-old claret or burgundy. After 1870, the life of the wines became shorter, and connoisseurs grumbled for years that the quality of French wine had been irrecoverably lost.

Some European vineyards managed to avoid the phylloxera pest, by the use of insecticides, and enormous care. Romanée-Conti was one of these. Then came the Second World War, and the insecticides were no longer available; phylloxera won the battle, and vines that had been planted by monks twelve centuries ago were destroyed. 1938 is the last year of the old Romanée-Conti, and there are probably very few bottles left in the world. The post-1945 Romanée-Conti is still a great wine, but not yet up to the old standard—if, indeed, it ever reaches it.

Oddly enough, the Americans themselves do not seem to mind the foxy flavour that makes many of their wines—especially those of the east coast—unpleasant to a European. I recall my own bewilderment on first encountering it. I was on my first visit to America, in 1961, on a lecture tour; one of my first stops, after arrival in Washington, was at Richmond, the old capital of Virginia. I was booked into a large and ancient hotel in the centre of Richmond. When I went to the dining room, I discovered that it was an enormous hall, with a balcony running round it. I had been placed on the balcony. The waiter lit candles in silver candlesticks; I sat there, almost alone in the vast room, feeling like Edgar Allan Poe pondering on quaint and curious volumes. I looked at the wine list; it seemed to consist mainly, if not entirely, of American wines; I decided to try the most expensive, produced (I have since discovered) by one of New York's largest wine firms. The bottle arrived; I believe it had a plastic stopper, but I may be wrong. I tasted it, and experienced enormous disappointment. There was obviously something wrong with it. I told the wine waiter so, and asked him to taste it; he said it tasted fine to him. I wasn't disposed to argue; I looked down the list, and chose a Californian wine. This tasted altogether better, although it was definitely a *vin ordinaire* (most American wines are undistinguished by European standards, although the better Californian wines are often at least as good as an ordinary Beaujolais). I told the waiter that if he liked the New York wine, he was welcome to drink it, with my compliments, and I paid for it on my bill the next morning. In retrospect I see that this was fair, for there was nothing wrong with the wine—at least, nothing that is not wrong with most New York State wines.

But to return to Vosne-Romanée. Not all its wines are to be compared with Richebourg or Romanée-Conti, but some of them are very pleasant indeed. When I became disappointed with the quality of the 1966 Chambolle-Musigny—as mentioned above—I spent a few weeks tasting my way through some of the other burgundies on the excellent list of our local brewery, until I came upon one labelled 'Vosne-Romanée—Les Suchots'.* There my search ended, I had found what I wanted: a wine of light and gentle quality, that can be drunk in the bar to wash down a beef sandwich. It was, I think, minimally more expensive than Chambolle-Musigny, but only just; and this is because the vineyard of Les Suchots is the largest of Vosne-Romanée—thirty-two acres, nearly half the total acreage of the commune. I gave it up only because I drank my way through the local brewery's supply.

South of Vosne-Romanée, we encounter the area that gives its name to the Côte de Nuits—Nuits-St-Georges. It produces a vast quantity of red wine from its 536 acres, most of which is sold as the commune wine, labelled simply Nuits-St-Georges. The commune has no great wines (*grands crus*), although it takes its name from its finest vineyard, Les St-Georges, which is a *premier cru*. I find most of the wines too heavy for my taste—the correct word, in wine phraseology, is firm—but for those who like their wine to taste full and round in the mouth, the commune wines of Nuits-St-Georges are excellent for everyday drinking. It has some superb vineyards which produce their individual wines (usually prefaced by the commune name—i.e. Nuits-St-Georges—Les Porrets); Healy mentions Les Vaucrains with special affection. I have never tasted any of these, so cannot comment.

We may say, as a simple generalisation, that the great wines of Burgundy are to be found in these areas I have so far discussed: the northern half of the Golden Slope. There are others; but in general, it is true that most of the remaining burgundies are straightforward, uncomplicated wines for everyday drinking. There are four main areas, going south: Beaune, Chalon, Mâcon and Beaujolais; all produce huge quantities of wine. The area that produces these covers thousands of acres, and stretches for another 125 kilometres to the south, beyond Villefranche. If you buy a bottle labelled simply Beaune,

* It must be emphasised that the '66 Chambolle-Musigny I found unsatisfactory came from a single shipper—whose name I shall not mention; others may have been excellent.

Mâcon, Beaujolais—provided you choose a reliable shipper—you can expect a decent quality *vin ordinaire*.* (You are unlikely to see a bottle labelled Chalonnais: they are little known in England or America.)

Beaune is still a part of the Golden Slope, its southernmost part. The wines, on the whole, are softer and lighter than those of the Côte de Nuits, and usually cheaper on wine lists. Faced with a fairly short wine list in a not-very-good restaurant, I would choose a Beaune as often as not—I mean, a bottle labelled simply Beaune. For many other well-known wines are also Beaunes—Volnay, Pommard, Aloxe-Corton, Meursault, Montrachet. The last two are among the best known of white burgundies.

Charlemagne owned vineyards at the northernmost end of the Côte de Beaune, at Corton. The wines of Corton are the only ones in Beaune that compare with the great wines of further north. Le Corton, Corton-Bressandes and Corton Clos du Roi, all possess more body than most of the Beaunes. Like most Beaunes, they mature quicker than the wines from further north, and possess a softer quality.

Beaune is a wine town; little else but wine-making and wine-selling goes on there. The Hospice de Beaune—whose name is connected with so many wines—is not, in fact, a hospital so much as an alms-house and charitable trust. Over the centuries, vineyards have been presented to the Hospice, and a great yearly auction of their wine is held in November. Part of the proceeds goes to the upkeep of Beaune's most beautiful building, the Hôtel-Dieu.

To return to Corton. The little town of Aloxe (pronounced Alosse) has followed the lead of other wine-producing areas in adding the name of its best known vineyard to its own. The commune wine is sold as Aloxe-Corton. I have drunk a great deal of it in my time; there was a period when I probably drank as much of it as of any burgundy. But with my definite taste for soft, light wines, I came to find it a little hard, and sometimes almost sharp.

In the same breath, I should mention another wine which, to

* By which I mean an everyday wine. In France, *vin ordinaire* usually means a non-vintage 'carafe wine'.

my palate, bears a resemblance to Aloxe-Corton: Clos de Conté. I have no idea where this wine comes from—probably the Côte de Nuits—and I can find no reference to it in any of the standard books on wine—even in the encyclopedia *Wines and Vineyards of France* by Jacquelin and Poulain; the only mention I have been able to find is in Maurice Healy, who also admits that he has no idea of where it comes from. It seems puzzling that it should be so elusive—until I reflect that France produces so many thousands of different wines that it would take an encyclopedia the size of *Britannica* to describe them all.

South of Beaune, the road passes Pommard, whose 1,750 acres produce 166,000 gallons a year. Pommard is perhaps the most popular of all the burgundies—certainly in America. (I mean, of course, French burgundies; the Americans call some of their own wines burgundy.) I drank a bottle recently in the local pub, so the taste is fresh in my memory—rather heavier than Volnay ('fuller bodied', as the experts say), and, to my palate, possessing a faint almondy-like flavour, as do some of the Beaujolais. (This may be purely a matter of taste; the Volnays are supposed to smell of raspberries and other fruit, but I have seldom noticed it.) When I lived in America between 1966 and 1968, I found that Pommard was often the only French wine obtainable in grocers', and even liquor stores; and on the east coast, where the alternative was usually a New York State wine, I preferred Pommard when I could afford it. The difference between Pommard and the native American wines was immediate and very striking; fuller, gentler, more roundly flavoured, somehow more civilised, although I am doubtful about the adjective. I also observed that the Pommard sold in America was often distinctly tired; no doubt the long journey and the American habit of keeping their liquor stores super-heated had sapped its vitality. Even so, past its peak, and costing more than twice as much as even a good American wine (say $5 instead of $2.50), I indulged myself whenever I felt I deserved a relaxing evening with a book or pile of gramophone records. The popularity of Pommard in America may well be due to its ability to take rough treatment on the voyage; it is longer lasting than most of the wines of Beaune (for, as already commented, most wines of Beaune mature fairly quickly). And it definitely possesses more quality, or elegance, than Aloxe-Corton, which, to my palate, has much in common with Pommard.

This is perhaps the place to comment that, next to leaving a wine exposed to the air, change of temperature is the chief cause of deterioration in wine. A few years ago I was driving my family through Scotland—I shall have more to say of this trip when I speak of whisky—and we crossed from Kyle of Lochalsh to Kyleakin on the car ferry; Kyleakin is, of course, the port of southern Skye. We booked in at a small hotel, and when opening time arrived, I went down to the bar and asked if I could see the wine list. The barman looked a little bewildered, but he handed me one. I asked for a bottle of Pommard. It arrived five minutes later, and once we had established that I wanted to drink it there and then, and not with my dinner (which again struck him as odd), he opened it. It was pure vinegar. I felt sorry to cause complications, and if it had been less awful, I'd have gagged it down; but I offered the barman a taste, assuring him that even if he had never tasted wine, he would be able to tell that there was something wrong with it. He agreed gloomily that it tasted like vinegar, and went off to get the proprietor—or manageress—a personable and efficient-looking young woman. With a resigned look, she said: 'Ye'd better come and see f'r y'rself', and led me to the 'wine cellar'; this proved to be a small room, the size of an ordinary larder. I half expected to find that the wine was kept upright in crates, but it was in racks, and there seemed to be a fair amount of it. Then she switched on the light, and I saw what was wrong. The small window was closed, and the light bulb was a 150-watt. It only had to be left on for half an hour, with the door closed, and the temperature inside shot up fifty degrees. Then they would lock up for the night, someone would switch off the light, and the room was soon cool again.

The Pommard, I saw, was stored above the level of the bulb. I selected a bottle of something from floor level—probably a claret—and it proved to be excellent. I explained the trouble to the manageress, but since we left the next day, I have no means of knowing whether the quality of the wine has improved.

About a kilometre south of Pommard, slightly off the road, is the village of Volnay, whose wines are the most delicate of the whole Côte de Beaune—perhaps of the Côte d'Or. The very word Volnay arouses nostalgia in me; it brings back memories of the year 1956. For it was in the June of that year that the late Esmé Percy—a fine actor and a most lovable man—took me to the Henekey's bar in Marylebone High Street to meet some of his friends, most of whom worked for a small record company in nearby George Street called Argo.

That upstairs bar of Henekey's was virtually a club. It was there that I first tasted that fine, delicate flavour of Volnay; we drank it by the bottle, each buying a bottle in turn. After the first occasion there—with Esmé—I found that I enjoyed myself so much that I often dropped in around lunch time. This was, I suppose, the first communal drinking I had done in my life—if you exclude the occasional late-night party—and I was amazed how pleasant it was.

They were not heavy drinkers, in the normal sense of the word; I suppose most of us got through a bottle each. No doubt it affected me more than the others, being less used to it. The room took on a rosy glow—I apologise for the cliché, but it describes it exactly—and I felt amazed that life could be so pleasant. I continued to be a lunch-time regular at Henekey's until I left London six months later to move to Cornwall; and then I was lucky enough to encounter the same relaxed good fellowship in the back room of the General Wolfe in St Austell; of this I shall speak later.

I no longer drink Volnay with the same frequency although it always revives pleasant memories when I do. And apart from this sentimental preference, the wines of Volnay are among the best in the Côte de Beaune—the most distinguished, as a wine expert would say. If it is true that the Beaunes are somewhere between the big wines of the northern Côte d'Or and the lighter wines of Beaujolais, then Volnay is just about the ideal median. It is understandable that it should have been the most popular wine of Burgundy in the fourteenth century, when the Knights of Malta owned many of the vineyards. Fortunately, its 1,100 acres mean that there is a quantity with some relation to the demand, so that the wine is not expensive. (Lichine gives

527 acres, which conflicts with the figure in the more authoritative Jacquelin and Poulain.) About a quarter of this output belongs to the *premier cru*, and these wines will be sold with the name of the vineyard on the bottle: Volnay-Les Mitans, Volnay-La Barre, and so on. The best comes from the highest vineyard, Les Caillerets. Wines from the dozen or so vineyards of the *deuxième* and *troisième crus* are generally sold simply as Volnay.

Of the remaining red wines of the Côte de Beaune that I have tasted, I can recall only Monthélie and Santenay. I remember the Monthélie not so much for any remarkable qualities of flavour as because it struck me as cheap for a wine of good quality, and this is something I have borne in mind ever since. I am not sure why it is reasonably priced, for a glance at a reference book reveals that the acreage of the vineyard is a mere 250; reasonable, to be sure, but only a seventh of the area of Pommard, which is more expensive and often less good. The same is true of Santenay, the southernmost village of the Côte d'Or, a soft, light wine which sometimes has a slightly earthy taste; not highly distinguished, but good value.

It remains only to mention the two great white wines of the Côte de Beaune: Montrachet and Meursault. I admit freely that I do not drink French white wines every day, or even every month; if I am going to drink a white, I prefer Moselle, with its touch of sweetness and an almost lemony tartness. If I am eating in a restaurant, particularly if the main course is lobster or salmon, then I drink the white wines of Burgundy. Of these, the greatest is generally admitted to be Montrachet, a mere seven-and-a-half acres. It is a superb wine, with a light and clean texture, dry and rather almondy. The best Montrachets (labelled Puligny-Montrachet) are clear in colour; the yellowy ones have less finesse. It is also, of course, rather expensive, and most wine drinkers might well feel that something less aristocratic does just as well to wash down a Dover sole. In which case, they may go for Meursault—readers of Camus will remember that he chose the name for the hero of *L'Etranger*, where it seems to signify 'death leap'. It should have a yellow colour—indeed, it may have a green-gold that recalls Wagner's Rhinemaidens or Kingsley's water babies—and a rich flavour, which has been compared to ripe peaches and hazelnuts.

If I am drinking a white burgundy at home with a fish dinner, or to wash down some of the excellent Cornish crab, I drink ordinary Chablis, supplied by the Wine Society. I have not mentioned Chablis so far, although I should really have begun with it, since we are moving from north to south. The Chablis area stands on its own, some hundred kilometres closer to Paris than Dijon, near Auxerre. (The name always conjures up, for me, the Belloc poem:

> When Peter Wanderwide was thrown
> By Death himself beyond Auxerre . . . .)

Its output is enormous—300,000 gallons a year (although this hardly compares with Beaujolais' 15 million), all of it made from the Chardonnay grape, the white equivalent of the Pinot Noir, from which all the great red burgundies are made. There are, of course, great Chablis—Les Vaudésirs, Les Clos, Les Grenouilles—and many ordinary Chablis, which may be drunk in quantity, like Beaujolais, if your taste lies in the direction of dry white wine. There is even a Petit Chablis, which lies at the bottom of the list, and is very much a *vin ordinaire.* I first came across a mention of Chablis in Henry James's *The Ambassadors*, which I read at the age of sixteen—the scene where Mme de Vionnet has lunch with Lambert Strether, the small-town American who has come to France to rescue a young man who seems to be heading for ruin, and who finds himself increasingly in love with the idea of such civilised ruination; James spoke of the 'straw coloured Chablis', and I decided that it must be a very exotic drink indeed. Perhaps it is that literary association that still gives me a fondness for Chablis, in spite of my general preference for red wines.

While on the subject of white wines, I should mention Pouilly-Fuissé, which in recent years has come to rival Chablis as a favourite dry wine. This is actually a Mâcon—I shall speak of Mâcon in a moment—and, like Chablis, it may be regarded as a kind of Beaujolais among white wines, to be drunk young, and swallowed rather than sipped. This is not to say that it is a *vin ordinaire;* it has its own fine qualities of bouquet and balance. But you would need to be a fairly experienced wine drinker to be able to tell the difference between Chablis, Meursault and

Pouilly-Fuissé by taste alone; in fact, it stands somewhere midway between the two. It is reasonably cheap, since it is produced in even larger quantities than Chablis—350,000 gallons a year, compared to Chablis' 300,000.

Of the most famous of all white wines, champagne, I shall have something to say later.

If you look at a wine map of Burgundy—for example, in Hugh Johnson's *World Atlas of Wine*—you will see that the Golden Slope, which comes to an end at Cheilly-les-Maranges (a village that produces a little fairly undistinguished red wine), is only a small part of the area. A few kilometres south there are the three smallish districts that make up the Côte Chalonnaise. And then, to the south, stretching for a good half of the distance between Dijon and Lyon, there is the vast area that produces Mâcon and Beaujolais.

It is worth keeping an eye open for the wines of the Côte Chalonnaise on restaurant wine lists, particularly Givry, Mercurey, Rully and Montagny. These are not great wines, or anywhere near, but they are good and inexpensive. (I note, for example, that the cheapest red burgundy on the Wine Society's list for Spring 1972 is a Givry.) Mercurey is the best of them, and compares well with Volnay or Pommard. Givry is robust, but less interesting, and the same goes for Rully, although I am fond of its white wine. Montagny is an excellent white, pleasant if not remarkable, and best drunk young.

If there is little to say about the wines of the Côte Chalonnaise, there is even less to say about those of Mâcon and Beaujolais. I do not mean that they are poor wines—Pouilly-Fuissé comes from the Mâconnais, and many Beaujolais are memorable. But you would not arouse too much indignation among wine lovers if you said that all Mâcon tastes alike, and that most Beaujolais is just Beaujolais.

I have already explained that the Pinot is the grape from which all the great red wines of Burgundy are grown, and that the Gamay, while it produces larger quantities of wine, never makes a great wine. Beaujolais is the only area where it produces very good results. Much of Mâcon is planted with the Gamay, and the result is a good, sound, drinkable wine that tends to coarseness. There is a pub in Mevagissey, the Kings Arms, where I always drink Mâcon—because the proprietor always keeps a few bottles in for me. It goes down easily, and if I drank it in Spain or America, I would count it a good wine, for it has character, that bouquet and firmness that is found in all but the poorest French wine; but if I have been drinking a better wine earlier in the evening, it strikes my palate as slightly harsh. Mind, this is just an ordinary Mâcon, perhaps one of the inferior ones. The wines from the vineyards of Romanèche-Thorins (1,312 acres) are close to those of Beaujolais, and produce wines that are like Beaujolais. The best wine of Beaujolais, its only equivalent of the *Châteaux* and *Clos* of the Côte d'Or, is Moulin-à-Vent, the Windmill, and Mâcon shares this vineyard with Beaujolais, part of Romanèche-Thorins. As to the rest of the Mâcons, it is characteristic that Jacquelin and Poulain's *Wines and Vineyards of France*—a dictionary rather than a book about wine—is full of such comments as 'greater in output but of a less good quality', 'inferior to all the above. . . .'

As to Beaujolais, what is one to say? It is usually a good, uncomplicated wine, almost the French equivalent of Burton-on-Trent beer, light in quality, easy to drink. It is probably the world's most popular red wine, for its best qualities emerge when it is young, and anyone can appreciate them. The wine labelled Beaujolais-Villages is slightly more alcoholic, and of a higher quality, than ordinary Beaujolais—which applies, incidentally, to most wines with the word 'villages' added—Beaune-Villages, Mâcon-Villages. Moulin à Vent is also a stronger, firmer wine, and a deeper red, than most Beaujolais, whose colour reflects its light quality. (Beaujolais is less alcoholic than most French wines, with 10 per cent of alcohol compared to the usual 11 per cent.)

There are a number of other Beaujolais firms that are allowed to call the wine by an individual name—eight, to be precise; the ones you are most likely to encounter in England are Juliénas (the northernmost commune, whose wines are much drunk in Lyon), Fleurie, Brouilly, and Morgon. These are the aristocrats of the Beaujolais—or at least, the upper classes—and most of them improve in bottle. (In general, though, Beaujolais does not age well.)

In my own experience, there are two kinds of Beaujolais. A good Beaujolais has a strong aroma and a very distinctive flavour—difficult to describe, but immediately recognisable—fruity, a faint touch of almonds, sometimes even a taste that reminds me of newly baked, crusty bread. 'Ordinary' Beaujolais has no aroma, and no very distinctive flavour; if it is good, it simply tastes fresh on the palate. There is a fashion now for drinking Beaujolais very young—Alec Waugh mentions drinking a good Beaujolais at six months old—but I am not an enthusiast.

South of Lyon, the quality of the wine changes once more; we are in the Rhône country, and the wine again has that 'heavy' quality characteristic of the best of the Côte d'Or, although without the delicacy and distinction. This is, of course, the wine-producing area planted by the Romans—perhaps even by the Greeks who brought the vine to Marseille. Generally speaking, the Rhône wines have a high alcohol content (often as high as 12.5 per cent) and take several years before they reach their peak. The Rhône wine area also runs in a north-south direction, beginning at Vienne, and ending just south of Avignon, the temporary home of some of the medieval Popes; and also of the most popular of Rhône wines, Châteauneuf-du-Pape. In my younger days, when I simply knew that Châteauneuf was regarded as a good wine, I occasionally made the mistake of drinking too much of it, and soon recognised that it left me with a worse headache than most wines. This was partly the alcohol content, but also, I think, the heavier quality of the wine. Since then, I have taken care to drink it—if at all—in moderation.

My experience with the pink wine Tavel, produced on the other side of the river from Châteauneuf, was also unfortunate. Some years ago, Leonard Hibbs, one of my drinking companions in the Mevagissey area, discovered that well-chilled Tavel made an excellent drink for warm summer afternoons, and if I dropped in on him in the evening to listen to music, we had Tavel with our Beethoven. From the beginning, I found it a little too acid for me, and on the few occasions when I drank too much, it was likely to produce diarrhoea as well as headaches.

(Acid is, of course, the wrong word to use, since it implies a wine that has begun to turn; but in this case, it suggests my meaning better than dry.) I am not suggesting that Tavel is not an excellent wine, deserving its increasing popularity. It is probably the ideal wine to drink with a Lobster Thermidor, where a Chablis or Pouilly-Fuissé might be too light, and a red wine too strongly flavoured—that is, unless you can afford a Montrachet or Corton-Charlemagne. But for casual drinking as you talk or listen to music, I would not recommend it.

The other wines of the Rhône are less well-known in England. The northernmost area, the Côte Rôtie (Roasted Slope—it conveys something of the beating sun that gives the Rhône wines their strength) produces wines that are, on the whole, more delicate than Châteauneuf. The terraces on which the grapes are grown are so steep that all the work has to be done by hand; consequently, in these days of mechanisation, the vineyards are shrinking—a good reason for trying the wine if you ever see it on a wine list, for it may one day vanish entirely; it is by no means an expensive wine. Neither is the more famous Hermitage, the fourth of the famous Rhône vineyards. Saintsbury has some appreciative words to say of Hermitage, which he refers to as a burgundy (as indeed it is, basically). In 1886 he drank a Hermitage that was forty years old, and says that it did not show the slightest sign of age. He says: 'It was, no doubt . . . not a delicate wine [Saintsbury's Scottish wine merchant called it "coorse"]; if you want delicacy you don't go to the Rhône or anywhere in France below Gascony. But it was the *manliest* French wine I ever drank; and age had softened it and polished all that might have been rough in the manliness of its youth.' And Saintsbury's attempt to describe its flavour is as good as any in wine literature: 'The bouquet was rather like that of the less sweet wall-flower. . . . Wine slang talks of the "finish" in such cases, but this was so full and so complicated that it never seemed to come to a finish. You could meditate on it; and it kept up with your meditations. The "gunflint" which, though not so strong in the red as in the white wines of the district, is supposed to be always there, was not wanting; but it was not importunate, and did not intrude too much on the special Hermitage touch, or on that general "red wine" flavour which in some strange way is common to every vintage from Portugal to Hungary.'

Saintsbury is full of these references to forty-year-old wines; for, as I have already mentioned, wines in those days were allowed to ferment longer, and to accumulate more tannin; nowadays, for many reasons (but mostly because of demand), wine is made to mature quicker. This generally does no harm, but it means that most people will never quite understand what Saintsbury means when he talks about a 'full and complicated' wine. The vineyard, incidentally, derives its name from a real thirteenth-century hermit, Gaspard de Stérimberg, who became a recluse after taking part in the 1226 crusade against the Albigenses, one of the most violent and horrible incidents in French history. For the Albigenses, although labelled heretics, were simply a sect of early puritans (the term 'Cathars', the generic term for these 'dualist' sects, means 'purists'). In 1206, Pope Innocent III called a 'Crusade' against these 'heretics' (of whom the worst that could be said was they were harmless cranks—for example, they condemned sex, and would eat no food that was sex-begotten—meat, eggs, cheese). H. G. Wells waxes indignant about the Crusade in his attack on the Catholic Church, *Crux Ansata:* 'Every wandering scoundrel at loose ends was enrolled to carry fire and sword and rape and every conceivable outrage among the most peaceful subjects of the King of France. The account of the cruelties and abominations of this crusade are far more terrible to read than any account of Christian martyrdoms by the pagans, and they have the added horror of being indisputably true.' When the Papal Legate was asked how to distinguish between heretics and true believers in Béziers, he replied, 'Kill them all. God will look after his own'. Which no doubt explains why Gaspard de Stérimberg became a recluse, and planted vineyards on the slopes that became the famous vineyards of L'Hermitage. We may drink the wine, and be glad that he tired of the army.

Bordeaux

Alexis Lichine records that the wines of Bordeaux were first made popular in the time of the Sun King, by the Duc de Richelieu, who had been banished to Bordeaux. The Duc, like most Parisian noblemen, did not like claret; his idea of a good wine was (naturally) burgundy. Someone got him to try claret with an open mind by giving it to him with a false label. He liked it, and it became his favourite; this, says Lichine, was the beginning of its popularity.

A modern wine lover would find it hard to imagine anyone being taken in by a claret in a burgundy bottle. It is true that *some* clarets might resemble some of the lighter wines of Burgundy; but the taste is usually distinctive. However, it must be remembered that even in the time of the Roi Soleil, a French nobleman would have less opportunity to try a wide variety of French wines than any middle-class citizen of today. A French king of the seventeenth century travelled as far as Bordeaux to sample the wine of St Emilion which he had no opportunity to taste in Paris—how should he, when the land journey was long and bumpy, and few wines could stand such rough handling?

We should also bear in mind that it was not until the early eighteenth century that old wine began to be appreciated. Until then, most wine was drunk young. And since most of the wines of Bordeaux require at least five years to reach maturity (and many of them twice that long), the stuff must have tasted horrible.

Compared to the Burgundians, the natives of Bordeaux were lucky in their geographical situation. The Côte d'Or was too far from Paris to be able to sell its wines there; throughout the Middle Ages, the French kings had to drink the poor wines of their local vineyards—and the wines of Champagne and Chablis, which could arrive by waterways. But the city of Bordeaux, although sixty miles from the sea, is on a major waterway, the tidal Gironde river; and, as already noted in the previous chapter, it formed an early alliance with England when Eleanor of Aquitaine married Henry Plantagenet in 1152, and brought him Bordeaux (then a part of Gascony) as her dowry. Their children were King John and Richard the Lion Heart. King John may have had his disadvantages as a king of England, but the Bordelais had reason to be grateful to him, for he encouraged the wine trade, and subsidised the planting of vineyards on land that was marshy. For three hundred years, Bordeaux remained English—to the irritation of the French king; and France continued to be partly English until the time of Joan of Arc and Charles VII. (It should also be borne in mind that Burgundy itself remained a separate country, ruled by its own dukes, until 1477.)

For a considerable part of its history, this wine of Bordeaux has been known as Graves—a name now applied only to one area—because of its deep gravel soil. It might be supposed that such soil would be bad for grapevines; in fact, by the time the vine has penetrated twenty or thirty feet of gravel to find nourishment, it has also acquired a certain virility which is reflected in its fruit; at least, that is my own view of the matter. For the wines produced by this gravelly soil are distinctly superior to the wines from the marshy lands (*palus*)—planted with the encouragement of King John—and the clayey and calcareous hillsides.

The nearness of England to the Gironde explains the long-standing popularity of claret in England. While Gascony belonged to England, everybody could afford to drink its wines—at least, everybody who could afford to drink. Later, the price rose; but even so, as we have seen, Shakespeare could have bought a gallon of good claret for under two shillings. At the beginning of the fifteenth century, nearly four million gallons of Bordeaux wine poured down the throats of the English every year, and in the age of Queen Elizabeth, this increased to fifteen million. William of Orange raised the duty on French wine to two shillings and one penny a gallon, which was more than a gallon had actually *cost* in Shakespeare's time, and thereby dealt the Bordelais a severe blow, although they had by this time begun to sell much of their output to the Dutch (who in turn re-exported most of it). A detailed account of the ups and downs of the wine trade will be found in André Simon's *History of the Wine Trade in England*—that great master's first book—and in the best modern book on Bordeaux wines, that by Edmund Penning-Rowsell.

By this time, the English were calling their Gascon wine 'claret' (*clairet*—clear wine). Creighton Churchill offers the cynical explanation that this was a scheme intended to exploit the English by offering them a blend of the good wine with the less good, 'somehow persuading the gullible islanders that a fine

Médoc or a lusty St Emilion, rendered milder and lighter by having been mixed with something else, would be an even more desirable drink than the original'. This could be true. But it is well to bear in mind that the 'lusty Médoc or St Emilion' would have tasted pretty harsh when drunk young, and the lighter, clearer colour of *clairet* may have been the least of its attractions. It should also be remembered that the other wines that were easily available to the English from an early date were Rhine wine and the wines of the Loire—the region a hundred miles or so north of Bordeaux; and both these regions produce light wines with a touch of sweetness. And, as anyone who has drunk Spanish or Portuguese wine in their country of origin knows, these wines also have a light and rather sweet quality. The English palate was conditioned to lightness. No further explanation of the popularity of claret is necessary.

At this point, I must explain that there is no quick and easy way to discuss the wines of Bordeaux. Burgundy is relatively simple. Once you know the five main divisions, running from north to south—Côte de Nuits, Côte de Beaune, Chalon, Mâcon, Beaujolais—you have a straightforward picture of Burgundy. But, as a glance at the map of Bordeaux will show you, there are at least nine main areas, spread around the two rivers, the Dordogne and the Garonne. However, there are five regions of Bordeaux that produce its greatest wines: Haut-Médoc, Graves, Sauternes, St Emilion and Pomerol. Of these, the Haut-Médoc (whose wines are called simply Médoc) is Bordeaux's equivalent of the Côte de Nuits. Most of the great wines come from this area.

Now Bordeaux is even more bewildering than Burgundy as far as the sheer number of its wines is concerned. There are more than two thousand vineyards. And, as in Burgundy, a vineyard producing a great wine may be on the other side of the road from one that produces an indifferent or downright poor wine. No one knows quite why this should be so; perhaps vines develop a kind of tribal patriotism. In Beaujolais or Mâcon this hardly matters, for the differences are so unimportant that it would not really make much difference if all the red wine produced in one year was placed in a gigantic vat and then simply bottled as Beaujolais or Mâcon. In Bordeaux, as in the

Côte d'Or, it would make all the difference in the world. So from a fairly early stage, some kind of rough classification was introduced—probably from the mid-eighteenth century. But it was in 1855 that the wine merchants of Bordeaux got together, and produced a list of wines, in five different groups (or growths—*crus*), with two subsidiary categories for bourgeois wines and artisan wines. (There was also a time when there was a classification of peasant wine, which must have been almost vinegar.) There were only four wines in the first growth, Lafite, Margaux, Latour, Haut-Brion. In 1973 Mouton-Rothschild was finally admitted to the top category. There were another fifty-eight wines in the remaining four classes. On the whole, this classification has remained unchanged—although it must be said at once that a wine of the fifth growth does not mean a fifth-rate wine. Perhaps because the quality of the wines has changed over the years, this ordering in *crus* is now almost meaningless. Everyone who has written about claret has given examples of a superb bottle of the fourth or fifth growth that deserves to be ranked with Lafite or Mouton-Rothschild. On the whole, it is best to accept the table of *crus* as 'a table full of exceptions', as Lichine puts it.

The number five seems to have some significance in the world of wines; not only are there five *crus* and five classic wine-growing areas of Bordeaux; the major one, the Médoc, has five important communes, from which the best wines originate: these are St Estèphe, Pauillac, St Julien, Cantenac and Margaux. I am taking them, as usual, from north to south. It is also generally true to say that the wines tend to be harder in the north, and to become softer and more delicate as one goes south. A St Estèphe may be an excellent wine, but even in these days of accelerated maturing, it is as well to choose one that is more than five years old; a young St Estèphe may be harsh. These wines are sturdy, slightly earthy in flavour, a baritone among wines.

You may often see a bottle labelled St Estèphe but it is altogether rarer to see a bottle labelled Pauillac. The reason is that Pauillac is so full of distinguished names that there are not many wines left over for blending into a commune wine. Pauillac (a small town) may well be the most notable single wine-producing town in the world, for within its commune lie the vineyards of Château Lafite, Château Latour, Château Mouton-Rothschild, Pichon-Longueville, Lynch-Bages, Pontet-Canet, Batailley, Puy-Lacoste, and several other names to bring a gleam to the eye of the wine lover. It is, of course, the only commune to have two of its wines in the *premier cru*, Lafite and Latour; although a third, Mouton-Rothschild, is now there too.

Those two aristocrats, Lafite and Latour, owe their pre-eminence to wealth and the care it can afford. Before the Revolution, both belonged to the Ségur family—Alexandre de Ségur was the counsellor of Louis the Fourteenth. Later on, Lafite was sold to a Rothschild for nearly half a million pounds, an incredible sum in 1868. Both wines are made from the classic grape of the Bordeaux region, the Cabernet Sauvignon, which is small and tough-skinned, and which gives the wine its breeding. Other grapes are blended with this to give softness—notably the Merlot and Petit Verdot. (Mouton-Rothschild uses a larger quantity of the Cabernet Sauvignon, so its wines are less delicate and soft—in fact, they are downright robust, and age superbly.) Latour was discussed by Montaigne in his *Essays*; Lafite was drunk by Madame de Pompadour and Madame DuBarry. The quality of the wines is generally described as elegance or finesse; they are delicate and balanced. Latour is sturdier than Lafite, and tends to hardness and astringency when young.

But although these three are the great Pauillacs, almost any bottle whose label says *vin de Pauillac* is worth investigating. Pichon-Longueville is the only Pauillac in the second growth; it comes in two varieties: Pichon-Longueville-Lalande and Pichon-Longueville-Baron, both good, full-bodied wines, although Lalande is more delicate than Baron. After this, most of the Pauillacs are fifth growths, but most are interesting. Maurice Healy has warm words of praise for Pontet-Canet, which, he says, has some of the breed of its near neighbour Lafite. The curiously-named Lynch-Bages (Mr Lynch was an Irish mayor of Bordeaux) is another fifth growth whose quality has caused an increased demand—and increased prices. Grand-Puy-Lacoste is another, and Grand-Puy-Ducasse, while less remarkable, is close to it in quality. There *are* Pauillacs that are fairly ordinary—Batailley, Croizet-Bages, Dauzac—yet all have the quality of Pauillac, a sturdy robustness, and many experts have declared that they deserve a higher rating. On the whole, then, the general rule is that if you don't know the names of the various châteaux on a wine list, you will be safe with any wine from Pauillac.

The next commune on our southward route is St Julien, probably the best known of the Médoc regions, and once again, the wines lighten in quality. It is strange, but there *is* an immediate change of quality. Maurice Healy remarks: 'Between the parishes of St Julien and Pauillac there is hardly a visible boundary, although if you look closely you will find a thread of a stream running between the vineyards of Léoville and Latour; yet there is *some* difference of soil, and Léoville is always recognisable as a St Julien and Latour as a Pauillac.'

The commune's full name is St Julien Beychevelle, and Château Beychevelle is its best known wine, with Château Talbot a close second. Yet oddly enough, these are both fourth growths, while the commune possesses no less than five seconds, including three Léovilles—Poyferré, Les Cases and Barton. Healy sings the praises of Poyferré, but that was in the thirties, and the quality of the wine deteriorated in the forties and fifties, although it seems to be recovering slowly. Of the three, Barton now has the highest reputation. Gruard Larose is a heavier wine, big and fruity at its best, but closer in quality to the Pauillacs than the typical delicate wines of St Julien. On the other hand, Ducru-Beaucaillou *is* a typical St Julien, whose quality has been rising steadily in recent years; it adjoins Beychevelle, and has many similarities—the same velvety excellence at its best. Langoa-Barton, a neighbour of Léoville-Barton, is another popular wine in England, but is not of quite the same quality as its neighbour. Lagrange, a third growth, is an example of a St Julien that does not deserve its high rating; it tends to be coarse, the kind of wine that could be bottled simply as St Julien. Incidentally, it is worth bearing in mind that most wines sold abroad simply as St Juliens are probably nothing of the sort; the commune does not make enough wine to produce large quantities of such a wine. Now that this country has joined the

Common Market French *Appellation Contrôlée* laws apply here, and unscrupulous shippers will have to unload their mock St Julien in America. (If, of course, before entry the bottle had *stated* that it was *Appellation Contrôlée*, then it was a different matter.)

As to Beychevelle and Talbot, already mentioned, the popularity of these wines may be due to the fact that they are under-classified as fourth growths, so that most writers on wine go out of their way to say what excellent wines they can be. Talbot is another big wine (i.e. heavier than most St Juliens); Beychevelle is lighter, but also more variable; harsh when young, it can become magnificent—Youngman Carter talks of 'silk velvet'; but it has had some poor years since the war.

Passing south again, we encounter Margaux and Cantenac, which may be considered together, since the latter is often hyphenated with Margaux. Château Margaux itself is regarded by many as the greatest of all clarets, and it is certainly among them. It possesses the quintessential claret qualities, the feminine delicacy and bouquet, the lightness and breeding, that make it clear why claret is sometimes called the queen of wines, as against burgundy's king.

Between Beychevelle, in the south of St Julien, and Lascombe, in the north of Margaux, there is a vineless gap of twenty or so kilometres—reminiscent of the gap between the Côte de Beaune and Chalon—which probably accounts for the considerable difference between the St Juliens and Margaux. The northernmost of the Margaux is Lascombe, belonging to the wine authority, Alexis Lichine. In his great Encyclopedia, Lichine says of his own wine: 'Excels in finesse, and has an indefinable light Margaux bouquet, epitomising the feminine qualities of the Médoc—a bouquet that many have defined as reminiscent of violets. The wine matures relatively rapidly and has great staying power. . . .' He adds that it is the most popular château-bottled wine in the U.S.A. During my own stay in that country, I had no chance to taste Lascombe; the most popular Bordeaux in most liquor stores seemed to be Mouton-Cadet, a pleasant but not very distinguished wine. From somewhere or other, I received the impression that Mouton-Cadet was slightly sub-standard Mouton-Rothschild, like Carruades, which is a part of the Mouton-Rothschild estate. Penning-Rowsell says this is not so; Mouton-Cadet is a blended wine whose ingredients may come from *anywhere* in Bordeaux—which gives the bottlers a hell of a lot of leeway.

As to the rest of the wines of Margaux and Cantenac (their quality is very close), a glance at the list of clarets will show that most of them are unfamiliar names outside France: names that are difficult to memorise, like Rauzan-Gassies, Malescot-St-Exupéry, Marquis-de-Terme. The first is another example of a wine that now no longer deserves its 'second growth' classification; the other two are slightly heavier than most Margaux, but often of good quality. Château Palmer is better known, perhaps because its name is easier to remember; another typical Margaux (strictly, a Cantenac), it may be harder than most Margaux (although one authority calls it *tendre*), and possesses a quality that justifies its popularity. Brane-Cantenac used to receive a high classification, figuring next to Mouton-Rothschild, but it has also slipped in recent years; at its best, it is a fine, delicate wine; Cantenac-Brown, with which it is easily confused, a third growth, is a fuller wine, but is more constant in quality and probably a better bargain.

Margaux and Cantenac are not the most southerly of the Médoc communes: there is Macau, which produces Château Cantemerle, a wine at the bottom of the list of fifth growths, but which is deserving of a higher place. The wine owes its distinction to a M. Dubos, who bought it in 1892, and who went to the length of making a record, three times a day, of temperature, wind direction and barometric pressure, and the precise stage of ripening reached by his grapes. The price is still reasonable as far as good clarets go.

In this short survey of the Médoc, I have not mentioned a number of communes, which may be looked up in the more comprehensive books: for example, Listrac and St Laurent, both producing good but not remarkable wines of the St Julien type; there is also an area to the far north which was known as Bas-Médoc (although it was allowed to drop the '*bas*' during the war—foreigners tended to translate it as 'base'). Since I could not find a single authority who had anything to say about these wines (except Cyrus Redding, who says they have an earthy taste), I bought half a dozen bottles of Château La Tour de By, a wine of Begadan. The taste did not strike me as 'earthy', although a little harsh, like a young St Estèphe. It is undoubtedly a Bordeaux; you could not mistake it for one of the claret-type wines of Australia or California. But somehow heavy. It had a touch of distinction—which is apparently more than can be said for many wines of the Bas-Médoc—but I would not care to drink it every day.

The parallel between the Haut-Médoc and the Côte d'Or continues to hold, in the sense that the remaining wines require far less discussion. In fact, for practical purposes, the everyday wine-drinker could think of Graves, Sauternes and Barsac as producing simple white wines, and St Emilion and Pomerol as producing simple reds. The main qualification to be made here is that Graves also produces many excellent reds, most of which are unknown in England. The area called Entre Deux Mers—which is actually between two rivers—produces mainly an inexpensive but pleasant white wine, as well as a few reds sold simply as Bordeaux.

The only great red wine of the Graves district is Haut-Brion, which must be understood to include Château Haut-Brion and La Mission-Haut-Brion, a slightly lighter wine; La Tour-Haut-Brion is also a fine wine. Now that England is part of the European Economic Community, no doubt many Englishmen will find it worth their while to take the car ferry to Boulogne, motor down through Bordeaux, and bring back barrels of red wine to bottle in their own homes; my friend Stuart Holroyd did it earlier this year, and I helped him drink some excellent bottles of red Graves, although quite *ordinaire*. It is definitely a sturdier wine than Médoc; Maurice Healy used a striking image when he said that the wines of Médoc strike him as being like a glossy photograph, while the wines of Graves (the reds) struck him as being like the same photograph with a matt finish. (He calls the red Graves 'noble warriors'—slightly fanciful, and perhaps better applied to great burgundies or Rhônes, but again conveying something of their quality.) The only other red Graves I have drunk (to my knowledge) have been Smith-Haut-Lafite and La Tour Martillac, both slightly heavy for my taste, but excellent. Haut-Bailly and Domaine de

Chevalier are also worth looking out for. But I note that on the Wine Society's list for 1972, with about sixty clarets on offer, there is not a single red Graves, a sign of how little demand there is for it in this country. Martillac, incidentally, is an area, and I seem to recall drinking at some time a good red wine labelled simply Martillac.

White Graves is frequently a sweet wine. In my early twenties, when I lived in London, I discovered Henekey's in the Strand, which sells wine by the glass; and, in my total inexperience, I found I much preferred sweet wines—Marsala, Madeira, Sauternes and Graves. I suspect many wine drinkers start in the same way. It was in this Henekey's that I first got drunk, on a mixture of Sauternes and Graves.

I should add that although I see no particular harm in getting drunk (particularly if you can stay in bed the next day), I feel strongly that it should be an accident that takes place in the company of friends, preferably not more than twice a year. Up to a certain point, alcohol produces a warm glow, an increased interest in life; beyond this point, it produces no new effect except a lack of co-ordination. To go beyond this point because you are enjoying the conversation and forget to stop drinking, seems to me reasonable, if undesirable. To go beyond it knowingly seems to me as absurd as overeating to make yourself feel sick.

But to return to the wines of Graves. For years after this early experience, I dismissed the white wines of Graves as rather sickly, fit only to be drunk with strawberries and cream, if you like that kind of thing. But about ten years ago I bumped into the writer Denys Kilham Roberts in a local pub—he was in Cornwall on holiday—and accepted a glass of the Graves he was drinking, Château Olivier. It was wholly a pleasant surprise: dry, but not as dry as Chablis or Pouilly-Fuissé; not unlike a Moselle, yet obviously a French wine. Since then I have occasionally experimented with other dry Bordeaux white wines, and found Entre Deux Mers, well chilled, of a pleasant quality that can be as easy to drink as Beaujolais. This is also true of Muscadet, a white wine of the Loire, which is dryer than Entre Deux Mers, and also lighter. Two other excellent Chablis-type wines of this area are Sancerre and Pouilly-Fumé, both with a flinty dryness. On the other hand, Vouvray, a sparkling wine, is sweetish, and can substitute for champagne.

If it is a popular error to think of Graves as a sweet, white wine, the description certainly applies accurately to the wines of Sauternes and Barsac. The extreme sweetness is obtained by allowing the grapes (mostly the Semillon) to become over-ripe, until they are slightly shrivelled, and there is a light mould on the skin. The result is one of the world's greatest sweet wines—perhaps its only great sweet wine (although I have tasted some nectar-like hocks). Good Sauternes is expensive, because it takes so many grapes to make so little, and the *premier grand cru*, Château d'Yquem, is the most expensive of all. (There are also five first growths and five seconds.) It has always been greatly appreciated: in the last century a Russian grand duke bought four barrels for nearly a thousand pounds a barrel—which, at 288 bottles per barrel, works out at somewhat over £3 a bottle. (The Russians have a sweet tooth where wines are concerned; on a trip to Leningrad in 1960, I found it hard to get even a dry red wine; the Russians drank with relish some horrible red sweet stuff from Georgia. In the last century, the Russians were one of the world's greatest customers for sweet champagne.)

Entre Deux Mers I have already mentioned; it produces huge quantities of a pleasant minor wine that could easily be sold in unlabelled carafes to go with fish or lobster. The region has no *châteaux* or famous vineyards. And crossing the Dordogne river to the east, we encounter St Emilion, whose wines are almost the red equivalent of Entre Deux Mers. They are heavier than the wines of the Médoc (except, perhaps, St Estèphe), good, satisfying wines that have something in common with burgundy. Within the past few days, I have drunk a bottle labelled simply St Emilion and a bottle labelled simply Médoc, so the difference is fresh on my palate. The Médoc, shipped by Louis Eschenauer, was a good, light wine that went excellently with a Chinese meal; the bouquet had a touch of almond, reminding me of the Italian Valpolicella; under different circumstances, it would have been almost too light, approaching a rosé. The St Emilion was less delicate, but was a big, satisfying wine that would have gone well with underdone steak. I felt that I could have gulped down two bottles of the Médoc to satisfy my thirst; I certainly could not have drunk two bottles of St Emilion, any more than I could eat two dinners.

St Emilion *does* have its *châteaux* and its classifications, but most Frenchmen would not take the trouble to learn them—the Bordelais have a rather casual attitude about St Emilion, as if it were a very minor wine. The best known is probably Château Ausone (named after Ausonius, the Roman Consul and poet of the fourth century A.D.), and after that, Château Cheval-Blanc. It is to Ausonius that Belloc refers when he writes (in the 'Heroic Poem in Praise of Wine') 'Awake Ausonian muse, and sing the vineyard song'. It is rather odd that Belloc should have a good word for Ausonius, for although nominally a Christian, he was very much 'the last of the pagans'. A professor of rhetoric at Bordeaux University, Ausonius was made governor of Gaul in A.D. 379, when his ex-pupil Gratian became Emperor of Rome. His closest friendship was with another ex-pupil, Paulinus, with whom he may have had a homosexual affair; later, Paulinus became a Christian, and rejected Ausonius as Prince Hal rejected Falstaff. Ausonius's poetic *Epistles* to Paulinus reveal the clash between the old Roman world, with its philosophic Epicureanism, and the new medieval world, with its life-denying Christianity. It would be appropriate if Château Ausone were one of the great wines of Bordeaux; but it is unfortunately a long way from being that. Cheval-Blanc comes closer to it. Of the other château wines of St Emilion, I have only tried Figeac, which I found to be heavy and rather 'earthy', typical of the virtues of St Emilion but more so.

Pomerol, to the north of St Emilion, also has several dozen *châteaux* in its *premiers crus*, and the quality of most of its wines lies somewhere midway between St Emilion and Médoc: fuller, softer than St Emilion, gentle, like the Margaux, but without their aristocratic distinction; in fact, if we are going to be fanciful, we could describe the Margaux as an aristocratic female, and the Pomerols as a plump and pretty barmaid. (The wine has a quality the French call *gros*, fat.) The best of them is Petrus. Anyone who dislikes claret because of the hard, alum-like taste of some bottles, will be perfectly safe with a Pomerol. Like St Emilion, it is made largely from the Merlot grape.

We come to the 'other wines' of Bordeaux. I have periodically explored the wines of Bourg and Fronsac in the Wine Society list, mainly because they are cheap, and have not been disappointed; neither had great character, although the Fronsac was a sturdy kind of wine resembling St Emilion or Pomerol, and Bourg was a lighter wine, closer to Médoc. Blaye, which lies to the north of Bourg, apparently produces large quantities of undistinguished wine, mostly used in blending; and the same is true of Cubzac, another large area south of Bourg. The area called Bergerac, well to the east of the Bordeaux region, also produces a number of rather ordinary wines. It is a pity; one would like to think of at least one good red wine being associated with the name of the great Cyrano; but the reds are very *ordinaire*, and the one well-known white, Monbazillac, is sweet and not quite as good as Sauternes. All the areas mentioned in this paragraph produce wines that are probably best drunk in their own local restaurants.

Champagne

As if Burgundy and Bordeaux were not enough to make France the greatest wine-producing country in the world, it has a third wine region, perhaps the most famous of all—Champagne. This is also the most northerly of the wine areas of France, lying some eighty miles to the east of Paris, and the weather is sometimes so poor that the grapes may be harvested only once every three years: only the first of the reasons that champagne is the world's most expensive wine.

Is champagne actually worth the money—that is to say, is it overpriced and over-rated? The wine experts all reply No! with one voice, but I do not find the matter so simple. It is true that, at the right time and the right temperature, even an inexpensive champagne can taste like Keats's vintage that has been 'cooled a long age in the deep delvéd earth'. That combination of the sharpness, the sparkle, the coolness and the aroma makes it one of the most thirst-quenching drinks in the world. On the other hand, I have recently tasted a Moselle that had the same effect on my palate; it was a slightly *spritzig* Kaseler Paulinsberger from near Trier, and although it cost only half as much as a fairly decent champagne, it was certainly not only half as good. The same thought has often occurred to me when drinking *spritzig* hocks and Moselles. Which certainly makes it arguable that champagne is overpriced 'for what it is'. What it is is certainly very fine and desirable; but still, in my own opinion, too expensive in comparison to other wines. After all, the expensiveness of champagne is due to the problems encountered in producing it which, as I have said, begin with the gathering of the grapes. (I think it was George Rainbird who commented that the grapes for producing one bottle cost about forty pence or one dollar.) Then there is the length of time of fermentation—from one to two years—and the problems of bottling and blending. When champagne was first made, the price was forced up by the high breakage rate, due to exploding bottles. That was finally overcome; and perhaps science will go on to overcome these other problems, and reduce the price of champagne by, say, a third—when it would, in my opinion, be worth the money.

The Champagne vineyards cover some 55,000 acres on either side of the River Marne; the total area is probably over 500 square miles, and includes the towns of Rheims, Chalons-sur-Marne, Ay and Epernay—the last two being in the heart of the great champagne area. This contains some thousands of vineyards, with over 16,000 proprietors, and the grapes (Chardonnay Blanc and Pinot Noir) are classified into *hors classe* and first, second and third categories. The shipper buys and combines the grapes according to the quality of the champagne he wants to produce. These are then pressed and fermented—the purple skin of the Pinot Noir being removed fairly quickly so as not to colour the wine. There are three pressings; only the first produces wine of top quality.

This juice is fermented in a vat—often after the addition of sugar (the process known as chaptalisation). After this, it is allowed to continue to ferment in a barrel. In December, some two or three months after it has been barrelled, the wine is racked, leaving the impurities in the barrel. A first blending takes place, to give wines from each town or area a uniform quality. Then back into the barrel for another two months, after which there is more racking. They may remain in barrel for anything from a year to two years. Then, in April, the long and delicate process of blending begins; the cellar-master has to determine, from the taste of the young, sour wine exactly what proportions will produce a good champagne. A little *liqueur de tirage* is added—cane sugar dissolved in wine, with perhaps a touch of citric acid—and the wine is now finally bottled. This sugar starts an artificial second fermentation in the bottle—special yeasts may be added. The fermentation goes on for three months or so, but the bottles are left in the cool cellars for at least three years, shaken periodically to prevent the impurities from solidifying into a lump.

This is the point where, in the past, the champagne makers found themselves confronted with a baffling problem. How do you get the sediment out of the champagne without letting out the gas too? The problem was first solved in the time of Napoleon by the famous Widow Cliquot who has given her name to a champagne. She invented a simple process in which the bottle is turned upside down, with its neck in a hole in a wooden bench. This is an extremely delicate process, known as *remuage*, and takes several weeks; each day the bottle is twisted slightly, to cause the sediment to slip further down, and placed slightly more upright. Eventually, the sediment ends on the cork. The cork is then quickly removed, a tiny quantity of wine is allowed to escape—with the sediment—and the bottle is resealed. Nowadays there is an even simpler process. The neck of the bottle is frozen and the cork removed; it comes out with the sediment attached to it in a piece of ice. The wine is given one final dose of sugar syrup—called *liqueur d'expédition*—and corked up, then kept for another year before it is ready to be sent out to the customer.

All this certainly explains why champagne is so expensive; whether it is worth so much trouble and effort is a question for the individual palate. The still white wine of champagne is not of any extraordinary quality (it used to be known as Sillery in mediaeval times). Healy records that during the slump, when the demand for fizzy champagne fell, a still champagne was exported; but it struck most people as a very commonplace white wine. (A small quantity of red wine is also made in Champagne. I have drunk it. It was a pleasant wine, heavy-ish, rather characterless, and probably worth exactly half the £2 it cost.) A cynic might say that the wines of Champagne had to be treated to make them palatable, just as the wines of Cognac and Armagnac taste indifferent except in their distilled form, as brandy.

In favour of champagne, it may be argued that it augments the party spirit by producing a gentle, glowing kind of intoxication. I say it *may* be argued; I have never noticed that the glow produced by champagne differs in any way from that of other wines. If I feel festive and relaxed, I would rather take a long, appreciative swallow of a fine burgundy or claret, at slightly more than room temperature, than of champagne. A couple of glasses of champagne at the right time—say in the early evening—can be superb; but my appetite for it soon vanishes. I notice that if I continue to drink champagne, the charm of the first two glasses vanishes; the continual assault on my palate dulls it, like listening to loud music for too long. It could be unsweetened lemonade. Burgundy or claret seldom has this effect, unless I am feeling liverish.

If I sound less than enthusiastic about champagne, I apologise; for on the rare occasions that I drink it, I enjoy it as much as anyone. I usually open a bottle on Christmas morning—or a couple of bottles, if there are enough members of the family present; and we all drink a glass, including the children. I have noticed on many occasions that champagne tastes excellent in the morning. (Schumann also thought so—champagne was his favourite drink, and legend has it that he occasionally drank it with his breakfast. But for a man with his tendency to nervous depression, this does not strike me as wholly a good idea; nothing is worse than feeling sleepy and dull at two in the afternoon.) I can also testify that a half bottle of champagne is a splendid drink in a pub on an autumn evening, when the landlord has lit a fire in the grate and the bar is still half empty. It is better still if you have a friend with you to help empty a bottle. But unless you are strong-minded, this can be risky; you feel so relaxed and interested in the conversation that you order a second bottle; and that is so pleasant that even before it is finished, you ask the landlord to bring up another; then your friend insists on buying another bottle to complete the round. I admit with shame that there was an occasion when two of us consumed no less than seven bottles (my friend, whose capacity was extraordinary, drank four to my three). But I regretted it in the night. That was the only occasion when I seriously suspected for a moment that I was going to die. I woke up in the morning with a headache, and a feeling of having been swallowed by a boa constrictor and then vomited up again; and thereupon made a vow that I would never again get drunk on champagne. When I felt strong enough to stand—at about three in the afternoon—I rang up my friend, hoping to find him equally feeble and broken-spirited; but he was unaffected. He said that he'd felt a little low towards midday, but that a whisky in the club had soon put that right. I brooded on the injustice for three days, which was the time it took my stomach and other internal organs to recover from the devastation.

I must admit that any wine, drunk in that quantity, would probably have a similar effect—although I think that the gas in champagne increases its potency. The moral probably lies in Maurice Healy's sensible remark that champagne is a great wine, and must be treated seriously; to drink seven bottles of anything in an evening is not to treat it seriously.

As a historical footnote, it may be added that Champagne may well be the oldest wine-growing area in the world; fossil vines dating from fifty million years ago have been found there. It was also one of the few areas in Europe to suffer under the edict of Domitian (A.D. 92) that provincial vineyards should be reduced by a half. The Romans were puzzled to discover that the excellent grape-growing soil was too poor and chalky to support wheat. It remains one of the mysteries of viticulture why this poor farming land, with its northerly climate, should produce such excellent grapes—the slope of the Montagne de Reims actually faces north. I would again suggest that this is a case of the grape deriving quality from the resistance it has to overcome.

A note here on this question of wine expertise. It is untrue that it requires a lifetime of study. All that is necessary, basically, is to know roughly what to expect from a bottle labelled Pommard, Givry, St Emilion, Pomerol. There may be a few experts in the world who can tell a wine by its taste alone, but I have never met one. Maurice Healy tells how, when he was in a Berlin restaurant, he saw a wine labelled Bordeauxwein 1927, and since he knew that 1927 was a very bad year for most clarets, he decided to try it; it was good, but too robust for a claret—whereupon the restaurant-owner admitted that he had had to blend it with a Spanish wine. Anyone who knows claret will know that this is no great feat. Most Spanish wines are closer in quality to burgundy or Rhône—some just taste like sweetish red ink—and the natural claret taste is as distinct from this as, say, a lime is from an orange. This comparison was chosen rather casually; but on consideration, I think it stands up well, for all Bordeaux, even Pomerol, has a flavour which is as distinct in its way as lime.

Again, Youngman Carter remarks, on this matter of connoisseurship: 'Only twice in my life have I seen a real expert announce correctly the name and date of a wine when it was served decanted, though I have often witnessed errors. In each case, the expert did it by a slow process of deduction based on knowing his host's cellar and anticipating the trap being laid; the nature of the wine, that is, the information he got from his eyes, nose and palate, had only half a share in the decision.' That is, he guessed by more or less unfair means.

This brings to mind one of the best stories about wine ever written—one I re-read every year with pleasure—Roald Dahl's *Taste*, and an account of it will make a fitting conclusion to this chapter. It concerns a rather disgusting wine expert who goes to dinner with a rich friend who prides himself on his cellar. The expert, a man named Pratt, plays on his host's vanity to persuade him to bet his daughter—against a couple of houses—on the outcome of a wine-guessing game. After which, he carefully smells the wine, washes it round the glass, swills it around his mouth before swallowing, and finally 'chews' it. His first comment is 'Um—yes. A very interesting little wine—gentle and gracious, almost feminine in the after-taste.'

When I say that this is a claret, readers should already be prepared to make their own guesses. It could be Pomerol, perhaps Petrus, but that is a fatter wine, not 'gracious'. You will probably suggest a Margaux, and you will be pretty close. Let us listen to Mr Pratt:

'Now we can start to eliminate. . . . First, then, which district in Bordeaux does this wine come from? That is not too difficult to guess. It is far too light in the body to be from St Emilion or Graves. It is obviously a Médoc. . . .

'Now, from which commune in Médoc does it come? Margaux? No, It cannot be Margaux. It has not the violent bouquet of a Margaux. Pauillac? It cannot be Pauillac either. It is too tender, too gentle, and wistful for Pauillac. The wine of Pauillac has a character that is almost imperious in its taste. And also, to me, a Pauillac contains just a little pith, a curious dusty, pithy flavour that the grape acquires from the soil of the district. No, no. This—this is a very gentle wine, demure and bashful in the first taste, emerging shyly but quite graciously in the second. A little arch, perhaps, in the second taste, and a little naughty also, teasing the tongue with a trace, just a trace, of tannin. Then, in the after-taste, delightful—consoling and feminine, with a certain blithely generous quality that one associates only with wines of the commune of St Julien. Unmistakably, this is a St Julien.'

The naming of the vineyard is also done by the same process of elimination—that is, by knowing by heart the classified growths of the Médoc:

'The wine is obviously not from a first-growth vineyard—nor even a second. It is not a great wine. The quality, the—the what do you call it?—the radiance, the power, is lacking. But a third growth—that it could be. And yet I doubt it. We know it is a good year—our host has said so—and this is probably flattering it a little bit. I must be careful. . . . Yes . . . I was right. It is a fourth growth. Now I am sure of it. A fourth growth from a very good year—from a great year, in fact.' The tannin taste offers a clue. 'Beychevelle . . . could it actually be a Beychevelle itself? No, I don't think so. Not quite. But it is somewhere very close. Château Talbot? Could it be Talbot? Yes, it could. Wait one moment . . . . No, I was wrong. It is not a Talbot. A Talbot comes forward to you just a little quicker than this one; the fruit is nearer the surface. If it is a '34, which I believe it is, then it couldn't be a Talbot. Well, well. Let me think. It is not a Beychevelle and it is not a Talbot, and yet—yet it is so close to both of them, so close that the vineyard must be almost in between. . . . Yes, I think I have it. . . . This is the little Château Branaire-Ducru.'

He is right. But the pay-off of the story comes when the elderly maid comes in quietly and presents him with his spectacles which he had left in his host's study . . . where the wine had been standing all day to acquire 'room temperature'.

A fine story, which illustrates the way that wine experts would *like* to arrive at their conclusions, but probably never do. In fact, looked at more closely, it doesn't really stand up at all. It would not be too difficult for Pratt to guess that it was a Médoc, simply because his host would be more likely to offer a Médoc than anything else. It is true that Château Margaux itself has more bouquet than any other claret (violets?), and that other good Margaux are noted for bouquet—Lascombe, Rauzan-Ségla, Rauzan-Gassies; but there are plenty of Margaux and Cantenacs that are less notable. For example, a Château d'Issan has a rounder quality that might deceive him into thinking it was a St Julien from the north, or even a Pauillac. (Beychevelle is, of course, in the extreme south.) As to his actual guess, Branaire-Ducru, I haven't tasted it in ten years and can't remember what it was like, but Lichine describes it as a 'sturdy', big wine, which doesn't sound at all like Pratt's demure but naughty female.

How, in fact, *would* a wine expert guess the identity of a wine? By somewhat the same process that I sometimes play a musical game with friends, trying to guess the identity of music on a gramophone record. There is the same process of elimination. 'That must be nineteenth century. French? It could almost be Mendelssohn. . . . But a touch of Tchaikovsky there. Russian? Could it be a fairly second-rate twentieth-century Russian? Glazounov . . .?' And you've got it. But there is no real elimination; you end by making an inspired guess. It could be miles out—it might actually be D'Indy or Chausson, or one of those odd Scandinavians, Gade, Svendson, Berwald. . . . And Pratt could just as easily have been miles out; it could have been a rather delicate Graves, a Smith-Haut-Lafite perhaps, or a fine St Emilion, a Château Ausone or Château Cheval-Blanc. The real point in knowing your wines is not to be able to identify an unknown claret, but to know something about the wine you are actually drinking: what to look for, what to expect. I think it is

Maurice Healy who says that half the pleasure of drinking wine is to talk about it, and this is true. If you are drinking a good wine, your mind should be on the wine and nothing but the wine.

THREE

Germany, Italy, Spain and Portugal

I HAVE MENTIONED that I prefer the white wines of Germany to those of France, preferably those with just a touch of sweetness. To my palate, most French whites lack distinction, and the distinguished ones—Corton-Charlemagne, Montrachet—are too much of a good thing for everyday drinking. A few years ago, I had a phase when I drank nothing but German wine. I liked it because it could be drunk rather than sipped. Of course, drinking with a meal is a different matter; you might almost say that the wine becomes a sauce for the food, and must be judged in contrast to the food. But if you are going to drink wine on its own, as you might drink beer in a pub, then it had better be something whose taste you enjoy. I discovered that I had a taste for German wine in 1957, when I spent some weeks lecturing at German universities. It was a very hot June, and I found that a large, well-chilled glass of hock or Moselle was the ideal thirst-quencher, better even than the excellent German beer. I remember camping near Coblenz, where the Moselle joins the Rhine, and we spent an evening in an unpretentious restaurant a few miles outside Coblenz, overlooking the Moselle—I believe it was at Winningen. I asked for the local wine; it was placed on the table in an unlabelled bottle. They told me it was a new wine—I can no longer remember whether they meant it was last year's vintage, or even more recent than that, but it tasted young and fresh. It was slightly *pétillant* or fizzy—the Germans use the lovely word *spritzig*, and English wine experts prefer to call it 'crackling', which is almost as nice—and dangerously easy to drink. I drank it from a large, round glass that probably held half a pint, and I drank so much that my wife had to drive back to the camping site. (Since that time, I have noticed that bottles of *spritzig* Moselle are often rather dry, and on one occasion, I had a bad tummy upset after drinking one—but that may or may not have been the wine.)

I was lucky; the tour, which had been arranged by the British Council, took me down the length of the Rhine, from Düsseldorf—where I drank the excellent beer—to Freiburg, and through some of the greatest wine country—the Rheingau, Rheinhesse and Palatinate (or Rheinpfalz). On the way back, we drove through Stuttgart and Würzburg—both in the heart of wine-producing areas—so that I can claim to have drunk most of the good German wines in their native areas. (I cannot make the same claim for France, for although I have driven from Dijon to Lyon, it was in a single day, and the amount of wine I consumed in that time was limited.)

The first thing I noticed about the German wines was how few of them resembled the stuff I was used to drinking in England, from bottles labelled Liebfraumilch or Moselblümchen. In fact, any hock can be labelled Liebfraumilch as long as it has pleasing characteristics. Most Liebfraumilch is a blend of hocks from the Rheinhesse region, and Moselblümchen (Little Moselle Flowers) is a similar mixture from the Moselle; to buy them is the equivalent of buying a bottle of French wine labelled simply Burgundy or Bordeaux. Bernkasteler Riesling is another blend of Moselles, from the Bernkastel region, reasonable in price (still, in 1973, well under £1 a bottle in England), and pleasant enough to drink, although, like any blend, it varies greatly from bottle to bottle. The wines I drank in German cafés and restaurants varied bewilderingly in taste, and in colour. They might be as clear as water, or golden, or even a yellowy-brown, like brook water in a district with iron in the soil. They might be almost odourless, or smell of a wide variety of flowers. The French are always talking about the various flowery bouquets of their wine, but it is usually so faint as to be hardly there at all. The German wines may smell quite positively of anything from new-mown hay to geraniums, and taste accordingly.

For me, it was a literary rather than an alcoholic pilgrimage. On the whole, I prefer German literature to English. (And I rate the French below both, although making something of an exception in the case of Balzac.) I have always loved the fantastic stories of Hoffman, Goethe's *Faust* and *Meister*, Novalis's *Heinrich von Ofterdingen*, Mörike and Kleist and Theodor Storm. (For years now, Broch's *Sleepwalkers* and Musil's *Man Without Qualities* have been my favourite bedside reading.) Later I discovered Rilke and Hesse and Wedekind and Thomas Mann. So in spite of the Hitler war (which started when I was nine), I had always thought of Germany with a kind of nostalgia, as a spiritual fatherland.

In a university bookstore in Cologne I bought some volumes of German novels in English, and I read through them as we drove slowly down the Rhine. The German romantics loved their own scenery, their forests and mountains and rolling countryside. This (from Eichendorff's *Life of a Good-for-Nothing*) is typical:

'Behind me [he is in a coach] disappeared villages, gardens and church towers; before me appeared fresh villages, castles, hills; below me crops, bushes, meadows; above me, countless skylarks in the clear blue air. . . . When the sun rose higher, heavy midday clouds arose on the horizon, and the air and the wide plain became so empty and sultry and still above the lightly swaying cornfields, and I remembered my village and my father and our mill, how pleasantly cool it was there and by the shady fish pond, and how very far that was now behind me.'

Not great prose, but evocative, and typical of the scene-painting of Hoffman and Tieck and Jean Paul. (The latter once immensely popular, is now forgotten, even in Germany; it is a pity, for he's an exhilarating writer, and his novel *Titan* inspired Mahler's first symphony.) What was so delightful was to read this kind of thing while actually looking down on just such a scene—the winding river, a church spire, perhaps a mill that might have been used as an illustration for Schubert's *Schöne Mullerin* cycle.

That great presiding genius of the romantic movement, E. T. A. Hoffman, drank himself to death at the age of forty-six, mainly on German wine, although he also had a predilection for a punch made of brandy, arack and rum, with suitable fruit juices. He once wrote: 'I associate Rheinwine with church music, Burgundy with tragic opera, Champagne with comic opera, and punch for a highly romantic work like *Don Giovanni*.'

It was the Rhine wine that he preferred to drink in his favourite cafés, where he held court and helped to direct the course of the German romantic movement for the next fifty years. He died some thirty years before his nearest American counterpart, Edgar Allan Poe, who also drank himself to death; but it seems somehow more romantic to ruin your liver on hock than on whiskey. And, unlike Poe, Hoffman did not drink simply to get drunk; he drank to escape the boredom of his life as a bureaucrat (he ended as a judge) and to stimulate his creative imagination. And the action of hock upon the system is so mild that it is easy to continue sipping it long after midnight, as the conversation takes a new turn. . . .

Writing of poor Hoffman—who deserves more pity than Poe because he was less spoilt and self-destructive—I find myself again thinking about that extraordinary and tragic century that destroyed so many of its men of genius. The writer or artist in the twentieth century is prone to think of himself with a certain self-pity; life is hard enough, and only a small percentage of lucky ones make an adequate income. But in the nineteenth century, there seems to have been hardly anyone who could escape the treadmill, even the highly productive ones like Scott and Balzac. The other day I spent an hour or so reading through an anthology of letters by composers—Mozart, Beethoven, Schubert, Berlioz, Wagner, Lortzing, Hugo Wolf, Schoenberg—and it was depressing to realise how many of them had spent their lives worrying about money, overworking for stupidly small sums. Hoffman, who was a composer as well as a writer, noted briefly in his diary for November 1812, 'Sold coat so that could eat'. And yet typically, the publisher of his first book (*Fantasy-Pieces in the Manner of Callot*) was a wine merchant named Kunz, and instead of money, Hoffman accepted a cellar full of wine. Not for forgetfulness, but because wine symbolises gaiety, freedom. All that the word claret symbolised for Keats, for example. Miss Marghanita Laski has investigated Keats's claret in an excellent essay.* It is obvious that he saw it as somehow synonymous with freedom; even in one of his last letters to Fanny Brawne, he is writing about the things he longs for: 'Trees, flowers, Thrushes, Spring, Summer, Claret . . . ',

* 'What Claret Had John Keats?' *The Compleat Imbiber*, 9.

and in another letter he suggests that his friends should drink a dozen bottles of claret on his tomb. Perhaps it was the name he liked, for his notion of claret seems an odd one. The 'blushful Hippocrene' he refers to in the *Ode to a Nightingale* is pretty certainly his claret—it is certainly not the water of the spring on Helicon he is referring to which produces a 'purple stainéd mouth'. In another letter he speaks of 'a little claret-wine cool out of a cellar a mile deep', echoing his 'cooled a long age in the deep delvéd earth'. But what kind of claret has 'beaded bubbles winking at the rim'?—i.e. is slightly *spritzig*? Miss Laski concludes, probably correctly, that what Keats drank as claret was probably a *vinho verde*—the Spanish term for a young wine—from Portugal. No matter; for Keats it symbolised romance, and the luxuries of life that he never achieved.

In fact, the wine Keats *should* have drunk was Moselle: *that* would have offered his palate the qualities he was looking for. You cannot really drink claret cool; this would be to lock up its true individuality, its bouquet. Whereas the essence of a Moselle —or of some hocks—is its assault on the tongue and palate. In David Lindsay's strange masterpiece, *A Voyage to Arcturus*, there is a passage in which the hero tastes the water of the new planet, 'gnawl water'. 'He found the water heavy, but bubbling with gas. It affected his palate in a new way—with the purity and cleanness of water was combined the exhilaration of a sparkling wine, raising his spirits—but somehow the intoxication brought out his better nature, not his lower.' I wonder if Lindsay had Moselle in mind when he wrote that. Vyvyan Holland wrote of Moselle: 'It should be served young at two to five years old, as against five to ten years of Hock, and at a temperature rather below that of other white wines, say at 45 degrees Fahrenheit. Moreover, it has a delicate and attractive flower-like taste which makes it an excellent drink for people of advancing years, who dread the after-effects of heavier wines; for it is non-acid, non-sulphurous and there is no tomorrow in a dozen bottles.'* Holland—a great bon viveur—becomes poetic and likens Moselle to a young girl, 'while hock is more like an older woman, with her more mature attractions'.

* From an article in *House and Garden*, 1963.

It was after that German trip that I began to drink German wines in preference to French, and the taste lasted several years. But I drank without much discrimination—Liebfraumilch, Bernkasteler Riesling, Niersteiner, without bothering my head whether it came from a particular vineyard or was a blend of a dozen or so wines. It was the novelist Rudolph Nassauer who undertook my wider education in German wines, for he also happened to be a partner in the wine firm of Nassauer Brothers. Rudi invited me to a wine-tasting party in his cellars near Charing Cross, under those great arches at the bottom end of Villiers Street, and there explained to me the basic principles of German wine-production. The Germans, with typical thoroughness, make sure that their labels contain all the information you might need. The label 'Hochheimer Hölle Riesling Spätlese Cabinet' looks bewildering, but it is easy enough to get the hang of. Hochheimer means that it is a wine originating in the town of Hochheim, which happens to be the town that gave its name to the wine—hock. (Until the nineteenth century, all German wine was called hock, whether from the Moselle or Rhine.) The next word on the label is the name of the vineyard near Hochheim—in this case, Hölle. Riesling is the name of the grape the wine is made from, the noble grape of Germany, the equivalent of the French Pinot and Cabernet. (You will not find the grape mentioned on most Moselle bottles, for all Moselle is made from the Riesling grape.) The *spätlese* means late picked, which implies that it will be sweeter than a wine without such a word on the label. *Cabinet* used to mean a wine specially prized by the owner of the vineyard—presumably kept in his own cupboard; now it is widely used to mean simply special.

Spätlese is the first of four terms indicating the order of sweetness and richness. The others are *Auslese*, *Beerenauslese* and *Trockenbeerenauslese*. The principle here is the same as with Château d'Yquem: that is, the grapes are left on the vine to become slightly shrivelled, but also sweeter. The owner is, of course, taking a risk, for he gathers the isolated, shrivelled grapes, covered with *edelfäule*, sometimes as late as December. These grapes have a high concentration of sugar which, providing there is sufficient acidity left, will yield a high alcoholic content which will preserve the great wines for twenty, thirty, even fifty years. In gathering the grapes so late, the owner has to gamble with the weather—rain would wash off the *edelfäule*.

I find that the chief trouble with a wine-tasting is that I end by wanting to take a dozen bottles of everything, and my pocket can seldom stand this kind of extravagance. But after that tasting in the cellars of Nassauer Brothers, I invested some seventy or eighty pounds in wine, varying in price from ten shillings a bottle to £5. This latter was superb stuff, a liquid nectar, and I must admit that buying it was absurd extravagance. I believe, although I am not sure, that this wine was an Erbacher Steinmorgen, a *Trockenbeerenauslese*. It was almost syrupy in consistency, like a liqueur, although perfectly clear in colour. It had a most delicate and fragrant bouquet, as delightful as roses or new-mown hay—Keats would have written a sonnet about it. The main problem was that there was no really suitable time to drink it. Ideally, I suppose, it would go with fresh peaches and cream, or some very special dessert. But at the time, my wife and I were living in a tiny cottage at the bottom of a Cornish valley. Cooking on calor gas, she would have found it difficult to prepare elaborate meals, even if she hadn't been also learning to cook by a process of trial and error (in a percentage of fifty/fifty). We ate our steak and chips off trays on our knees—a bad habit that has persisted—and since I seldom bother with a sweet—even now—it seemed somehow wrong to end the meal with a glass of a £5 *Trockenbeerenauslese*. I ended by drinking it after a hard day's work, when I felt I deserved some special reward.

Out of all the hocks I sampled, I ended with a strong preference for two of medium price: a Marcobrunner of Freiherr Langwerth von Simmern—one of the great names of the area, much as Rothschild is in Pauillac—and an Oppenheimer Krötenbrunner (which means Toad Fountain). The Marcobrunner (a Rheingau) was very slightly fizzy and definitely fruity or spicy, a delicious wine, while the Krötenbrunnen, a Rheinhessian wine, was lighter, but very delicate. I have always avoided the late-gathered wines—from *spätlese* upwards—finding them, in general, too rich for my palate. (The grapes for *Trockenbeerenauslese* are almost raisins by the time they're picked.) I observed in hocks in general that there is often a marked difference in quality from year to year, far more noticeable than in French wines. Rudi Nassauer, writing about this in an article (in *House and Garden*) said: 'Thus the '50s had a mustiness which was quite clearly discernible in the aroma and flavour of the wine. The '53s were fruity, elegant, robust, very fine indeed. The '58s were astringent, fresh, acidy, ideal dry wines. The '59s were perfect, indeed classical, inasmuch as they showed the highest standards German wines could reach. They had elegance, fruitiness, cleanliness and harmony.'

Drinkers of German wine should also bear in mind that, compared with France, German wine-making is almost a cottage industry. The French have three million acres of vineyards; the Germans a mere hundred-and-sixty thousand—not much more than a twentieth of the area. Moreover, only one-eighth of this total produces top-ranking wines. On top of all this, the German wine-grower has the problem of a short grape season, and the sudden onset of cold weather often forces him to gather the grapes prematurely. In that case, German law allows the grower to add grape juice to the must, allowing it to rise to its proper level of alcohol or sweetness. There are strict penalties about overdoing this. The word *Cabinet* on a label, besides indicating that the bottler considers it of special quality, is also a guarantee that no sugar has been added; the word *Naturwein* or *Naturrein* implies the same thing.

All things considered, then, it is not surprising that German wine-production is modest compared to that of France. Germany has to be a nation of beer drinkers. If all German wine was divided up equally among the population—including East Germany—each person would get two gallons every year. If all French wine was divided in the same way, each French man, woman, and child would receive about thirty-three gallons. Germany exports a mere four million gallons a year; France exports eighty million. And the French are such Gargantuan wine-drinkers that they actually *import* three times that amount every year from Algeria, Spain and other countries.

On the other hand, Rhenish wine has always been immensely popular in England, quite as popular as claret; and in the eighteenth century, it almost replaced claret in England. André Simon quotes an English doctor, William Salmon, who declared in a book published in 1693 that Rhenish wine 'is a good nephritic [easer of kidney pains] and vehemently diuretick, opening all obstructions of urinary parts, and bringing away stones, sands and gravel. . . . ' In the reign of Henry VIII it was a mere shilling a gallon, although, like everything else, it became more expensive under Queen Elizabeth. In the middle of the nineteenth century, a bottle of 'Old Hock' fetched the astounding price of twelve shillings a bottle—about £5 in our currency. This was obviously *Trockenbeerenauslese*. In fact, hock, because of its high sugar content, is probably the longest lived of all wines; Simon records that in 1961, a bottle of 1540 Steinwein was opened in the offices of Ehrmann's, the wine merchants (now owned by Rudolf Nassauer), and was still alive and very drinkable; on the other hand, bottles of 1822 and 1857 had *not* survived, and were simply dead—dumb, wet rags. An amazing thought, that a wine made a quarter of a century before Shakespeare was born should have been drunk in the year of the death of Hemingway.

The salient facts about German wines and the wine-growing areas are easy to memorise. Let me offer a short summary.

First, the Moselle, the charming river that joins the Rhine at Coblenz. The river winds and twists among some beautiful hill scenery—the ideal place for a wine tour. Much of the French wine country is downright dull; this does not apply to the Moselle region. It rises in northern France, and flows north-east, joined by two rivers, the Saar and the Ruhr. Consequently, all Moselle labels carry the words Mosel-Saar-Ruwer. In the main wine-producing part of the river, there are five principal villages: Piesport, Wehlen, Zeltigen, Graach and Bernkastel. I have already explained that a wine that merely calls itself 'Bernkasteler Riesling', without the name of the vineyard, should be regarded with the same suspicion as a bottle labelled merely 'Burgundy'; although, I hasten to add, it may be a pleasant wine, and even good value. If you are looking down a wine list, and you want to spend less than £1 on a bottle of Moselle, it is usually wiser to choose a lesser known name *with* a vineyard mentioned: Wiltinger Schlossberg, Piesporter Goldtröpfchen, Bernkasteler Küser Kardinalsberg; then, at least, you are getting an individual wine. The most famous single wine of the Moselle is Bernkasteler Doktor, which achieved its fame as the result of a recommendation by Edward VII's physician. The name is easy to remember, but it is not necessarily the best wine of the region. The Germans regard the Wehlener Sonnenuhr as the best of all Moselles, and I see that my Wine Society catalogue (in 1973) has bottles at £1.75, which is reasonable. It is also worth noting that a catalogue for 1968, four years earlier, lists it at 33/6 a bottle, so that it rose only 7½p in four years, a great deal less than most wines. Zeltinger has the largest wine production of the five villages. I would recommend the Graacher Himmelreich (Kingdom of Heaven!) and Wehlener Sonnenuhr (Sundial) as superb wines; its Schlossberg ranks among the great wines of Germany, another 'liqueur wine'.

But the Moselles remind me of a point I have already made in connection with burgundy: that there are so many hundreds of wines in each of the major wine-producing countries of the world that a man who knew them all would be some kind of freak or pedant. In the course of writing this book, I have taken every opportunity to taste wines I had never tasted before, and to make notes about them; but in at least fifty per cent of cases, I have been unable to find any reference to the wine in my own small library. For example, I have tried three wines of the Trier district (where Ausonius held his consulship)—which is regarded as one of the lesser wine areas of the Moselle. The Kaseler Paulinusberg was outstanding: delicious, young, *spritzig*, one of the best Moselles I have ever tasted (a 1970). The other two were enjoyable, but drier, stiller and less immediately striking. None of them is mentioned in any book on wine I possess. On the other hand, a bottle of a 1970 Maximin Grunhaus (from Mertesdorf, on the Ruhr), struck me as only a moderately interesting wine; yet Hugh Johnson mentions it as a product of one of the Moselle's supreme vineyards, owned by one of the world's best wine growers. The wine-lover who tried to regulate his drinking according to the textbooks would miss some excellent bargains.

*

I think of the Moselles as Germany's equivalent of claret, while the hocks are its burgundies. A glance at a wine map will show that by far the largest wine area is the great starfish-shaped lump south of Coblenz, with one tentacle reaching down the River Nahe, another reaching across towards Frankfurt, along the Main, and two more, pointing roughly south and north along the Rhine itself. This contains three important regions: Rheingau, Rheinhesse and Nahe. South of this, on the west bank of the Rhine, there is the long narrow strip of the Palatinate or Rheinpfalz; this produces the largest quantity of German wine. One is tempted to add 'and the lowest quality', but in fact, the best wines of the Palatinate are as good as anything produced in Germany; it is merely that it produces a vast quantity of very ordinary wine. These areas produce most of the wines that the foreign wine-drinker is likely to encounter. Of these, the most important is the Rheingau, Germany's equivalent of the Côte d'Or.

If you follow the Rhine from Coblenz to the south, you soon enter Rheingau (*gau* means district) territory; but most of the wines produced in this south-flowing part of the Rhine are only of medium quality. The town of Lorch is the largest wine-producer of the Rheingau, but nothing special comes from it. Bacharach, to the north-west of Lorch, was once one of the most famous of German wine-names in England, ranking with Hochheim. It is actually named after Bacchus. But its fame arose from the fact that it was a wine port, like Bordeaux, from which most of the wines of the region were loaded on to the big ships that would take them abroad. The big ships couldn't get further south, past Bingen.

But Bingen is the point at which the Rheingau begins to produce its great wines—the very point at which its course takes a right-angle turn, to run from west to east. (Bear in mind, though, that the Rhine is flowing the opposite way.) This is ideal wine-growing country, with its steep-sided valleys, protected from the east and north by the Taunus mountains. This German Golden Slope extends along the north bank of the river, from Rüdesheim to Mainz, and even further, to Hochheim (which is, strictly speaking, on the River Main, not the Rhine, and therefore really part of the Main area of wine production). The Hochheim wines have a slightly earthy flavour, but they are among the best and most typical of the Rheingau; its best vineyard is Domdechaney. The wines from Rauenthal are usually regarded as the finest of Rheingau, and are proportionately more expensive than most—although I have paid as little as £1.25 a bottle for them. I have already mentioned Marcobrunner as one of my own favourites, particularly the one from Baron Langwerth von Simmern's vineyard. The other classic wine of the area is Schloss Johannisberg, which used to be the equivalent of a first growth claret. I say 'used to' only because many other Johannisberg vineyards are now producing wines of equal quality. The English wine-drinker is likely to encounter the Johannisberger Erntebringer (Bringer of Harvest), which I have always found an excellent bargain if occasionally too sweet. Rüdesheimers, while pleasant, are not on the same level usually. Assmanhausen, between Rüdesheim and Lorch (i.e. just outside the 'great' area for Rheingaus) produces one of the best-known German red wines. Many people are not even aware that Germany produces any red wine, although Saintsbury has some kindly words to say of them. Assmanhausen is sweet, although grown on Burgundy vines, brought by monks in the twelfth century; Hallgarten says he once served it instead of port, and it was agreed that it was ideal for afternoon drinking, being less sleep-making than port. The chief German red wine region is the Ahr valley, far to the north, near Bonn; but although the wines are much drunk in Germany, they are not exported, for they are often like very ordinary burgundies, without the richness. They are, in fact, red hocks, but without the qualities of hock or of good red wine.

If we continue on up the Rhine, past Mainz, we now proceed due south for thirty miles or so, to Worms. This is Rheinhesse, or Rheinhessen, or Rheinhessia—the various authorities seem to disagree on what it should be called. Without pressing the comparison too far, you could say that this is Germany's equivalent of Beaune (while the Rheinpfalz, further south still, is its Beaujolais). This is mostly gentle, pleasant wine, seldom remarkable, and the best known in England is probably Niersteiner, the largest wine commune on the Rhine; its wines are always pleasant and drinkable, sometimes very good—the *spätleses* and *ausleses*—sometimes great. Wine-lovers will recognise many other names, from Bingen in the north to Dalsheim in the south, with such names as Bodenheim, Nackenheim, Oppenheim (which produces the Krötenbrunnen I have mentioned), Schwabsburg and Dexheim—the last three mentioned being regarded, with Nierstein, as the major wine-producing areas of Rheinhesse.

The best-known wine of Rheinhesse—regrettably—is Liebfraumilch, which could be regarded as the commune wine of Rheinhesse. It is named after the Church of Our Lady (Liebfrauenkirche) in Worms, although, in fact, only a tiny amount of wine comes from the very small vineyards around the church. Bingen produces one superb wine, Bingen Scharlachtberg (Scarlet Hill), whose *spätleses* and *ausleses* fetch top prices (say around £4 a bottle). Oppenheimers are generally conceded to be less good than Niersteiners—softer, but with less breeding—although they may be better than Niersteiners in hot, dry years. (Niersteiners share this characteristic with the Rheingau wines, that they seem to prefer gentler, cooler weather—for the Rheingau area is a kind of natural greenhouse anyway, with the river reflecting back the sun.) I should also mention Nackenheim, whose wines used to be used to make Liebfraumilch, but have improved until they are now sold under their own label, and Ingelheim, whose red wines are probably the best in Germany. Nackenheim and Alsheim, in part, have a red soil, like Devon. After a number of years in bottle, wines made in the great years reflect a tinge of red in the golden colour.

Moving west, for a moment, we should glance at the wines of the Nahe valley, which are sometimes regarded as a kind of halfway house between the Moselles and hocks. Many of the vineyards grow the Sylvaner grape—which is to the Riesling what the Gamay is to the Pinot—which flourishes and produces good wine in this area. The Nahe flows more-or-less south from Bingen, but until it reaches Bad Kreuznach, five or six miles south, the wines are hardly distinguishable from Rheingaus. Between Bad Kreuznach and Schloss Böckelheim, the wines are typical Nahes and of high quality; Niederhausen, which lies between them, also produces one of the best-known wines of the region, Niederhauser Hermannshöhle. Schloss Böckelheimer

Kupfergrube is perhaps the finest of the Nahe wines, while Goethe had high praises for Monzingen, further upstream.

Moving south from Worms, we enter the Palatinate or Rheinpfalz. The area itself is gentle and lovely, a place of orchards and pretty villages, warm enough in summer to grow figs, peaches, lemons, cherries, apricots. The wines are characteristic, with their own bouquet, but mostly pleasant rather than remarkable. Because of its mild climate and long summers, the area produces more *Beerenauslese* and *Trockenbeerenauslese* than anywhere else in Germany. All Palatinate wines share one characteristic: the flavour stays on your palate for only a moment, then disappears.

The Palatinate is so named because the Emperor Augustus built one of his imperial residences there. (Pfalz is derived from palast—palace.) The area is divided into three—the Upper Haardt (named after the mountains), Middle Haardt and Lower Haardt. (On the map, the Upper Haardt is at the bottom and the Lower Haardt on top.) The Upper Haardt, being the warmest, produces vast quantities of wine, and it would not be inaccurate to think of this as the hock equivalent of Beaujolais—drinkable, pleasant, undistinguished. In England or America you are unlikely to see any Upper or Lower Haardt wine with its own distinguishing label.

The Middle Haardt is a different matter. Extending from Neustadt in the south to Dackenheim in the north, it has thirty-two villages, of which sixteen produce fine wines. Five of these produce the best wines of the Middle Haardt (again, that number five, which seems to occur so frequently in speaking of wines). They are Deidesheim, Forst, Königsbach, Ruppertsberg and Wachenheim. Forster and Deidesheimer wines are generally reckoned to be the best, with a certain rivalry between them, but all five villages produce distinguished wines. I have said that a large percentage of these belong to the four categories of late gathered—heavy, fruity, flowery dessert wines. On the other hand, the town of Haardt, not far from Neustadt, produces a large number of medium wines (i.e., not of first quality—read 'ordinary') with the name Haardtherzchen on the label; these are very reasonably priced, and if the name were not so unpronounceable, I believe they might become very popular in

England. Finally, I should mention that Ruppertsberg and Bad Dürkheim produce red wines which are well known in the area, although not drunk much outside it.

These are the main German wine areas; I should mention, in addition, that the northern part of the Rhine, above Bingen, through Coblenz towards Bonn, is known as the Middle Rhine; it is extremely beautiful, but the wines are not to be compared with those of the Rheingau, Rheinhesse and Rheinpfalz.

And if you go in the opposite direction, up the Rhine towards its source beyond the Bodensee—Lake Constance—you pass dozens of small wine-growing areas, including Lake Constance itself; I recall with nostalgia driving down through Heidelberg, Karlsruhe, Baden, to Freiburg, and some of the excellent wines encountered en route. But the books on wine are oddly reticent about these areas, and Hugh Johnson does not even bother to mention them in his own book on wine, or include them in his wine atlas, which seems an oversight. I am quite unable to pronounce on them on the strength of a fifteen-year-old memory. Even the otherwise excellent Hallgarten dismisses them in a couple of pages of *Rhineland Wineland*, giving the impression that he has not tasted them. Next time I get to that part of Germany, I shall try as many as I can, and hope to include a section on them in some future edition of this book. It is probably fair to say that they are *vins ordinaires*, but I have often been delighted with the quality of a local wine. An example was a place in Switzerland called Aigle, amid splendid mountain scenery. I ordered a carafe of the local wine with the evening meal. It was red, and I can only describe the taste as rocky or perhaps flinty, a wine with a feeling of sturdy quality, but without any of the refinements. I was told that it was not sold much beyond the locality, probably because it did not travel. We took a couple of bottles with us, and I drank them the next day; they tasted as good as ever.

There are two more wine areas of Germany that deserve mention. All along the River Neckar, up through Stuttgart, there are smallholdings with vines—although no major vineyards. The climate here is so severe that the vines have to be taken down and covered with straw in winter. The whole area is usually known under the name of Würtemberg, and its wines are pleasant and light, with a touch of the Moselle. One of its pleasantest wines is the rosé Schillerwein, a lovely name meaning iridescent. Apparently this was first made when the vineyards were replanted after the Thirty Years War, and red and white grapes were mixed without much concern for pure wine. The Schillerwein is still a great favourite of the Swabians; but less of it is being made every year.

Finally, there is the area known as Franconia, rather further along the River Main, towards Hochheim, in the Würzburg area. The grapes are mostly the humble Sylvaner, and the wine is known collectively as Steinwein. (In fact, there are at least four major varieties, including some reds; but the difference in quality is not so great that this need concern us.) The best Steinwein comes from the Stein vineyard, near Würzburg. They are easy to remember because of their distinctive green bottles, the *bocksbeutel* (which some scholars take to mean a book-bag, others a goat's scrotum). These look rather like a crème de menthe bottle (with a sawn-off neck) which has been flattened in a vice. Most of the connoisseurs have a good word to say about Steinwein, but I have never understood why. To me, it is rather a feeble wine, drier than most hocks, but without the body of a Chablis—it makes me think of a Chablis that has been diluted with water or even a very dry cider. Because of its lack of body, I find it a good thirst quencher early in the evening—you feel it would be no sacrilege to add soda water to it. (The Victorians were fond of hock and soda as a thirst quencher, and John Betjeman's poem on the arrest of Oscar Wilde in the Cadogan Hotel mentions that he was drinking it.) It also goes well with fish meals.

There is a similar quality in many of the wines of Alsace—although the wide variety makes it risky to generalise. Because Alsace has changed ownership so many times, its wine industry has seen more fluctuations than that of Bordeaux or Burgundy. The Germans, when they have been masters of Alsace, have tended to encourage the production of cheap wine, partly to prevent competition with their own, partly to use it as the French use Algerian wine, to dilute the native product for everyday drinking. The Alsatian wine industry has now recovered from the damage of the last war, and large quantities are exported. (I have even seen an Alsatian Riesling on a British Railways menu recently—a better bargain, on the whole, than the Liebfraumilch and Zeltinger Riesling offered on the same list.) Quality has risen, but the chief virtue is still its cheapness—the prices compare with the Yugoslav Riesling. On a Wine Society list for 1969, I see that its most expensive Alsatian wine is a 'Traminer, Réserve Exceptionelle', described as very fine, which was, then, a mere 23/6d a bottle. (The Traminer is a grape resembling the Riesling, which ripens earlier, so in bad years, Traminer wines are likely to be better than Riesling.) For various reasons, Alsace wines are not *Appellation Contrôlée*, although their quality is controlled under their own laws; they are usually sold under the name of the grape—Riesling, Traminer, Sylvaner, etc.—and sometimes the town—Riquewihr being perhaps the best known. This latter is a dry, light, rather fragrant wine that I often drink early in the evening. It is probably true to say that most Alsatian wines should be regarded as everyday wines for quenching the thirst or washing down food.

I should add in parenthesis, while on this subject of hocks, that England is now, at last, producing a few of its own, three of which are listed by the Wine Society. I have tried all three: Anderida and Merrydown Riesling Sylvaner, both made by the Merrydown Company, and Hambledon, made in a Hampshire vineyard owned by Major General Sir Guy Salisbury-Jones. This latter has character, but I found it too dry for my own palate, somewhat resembling a Muscadet. Anderida, made at Horam in Sussex, is a pleasant wine, but without character. On the other hand, the Sylvaner Riesling—presumably made from those two grapes—seems to me to have some of the freshness and slight acidity of a Moselle, and a slight fruitiness more like that of a hock. All three wines are priced at slightly over £1, and cannot really be regarded as competitive with the cheaper hocks and Moselles; but it is a good sign that the English should again be trying to make their own wine. After all, Coblenz is roughly on the same line of latitude as Plymouth, and the Ahr valley, the world's northernmost wine-growing area, is roughly on a level with the centre of Sussex. What defeated the British in the time of the Romans, and later in the early Christian centuries, may present no problems for modern agricultural methods. I have even come across a book that states that in the eleventh and twelfth centuries, Gloucestershire, with parts of Kent and Ely, was the vineyard of England, and that the wines of England were then the equal of those imported from Bordeaux. An interesting thought, suggesting that England holds the world record for the most northerly-produced wines. But I am inclined to regard this as just another of those legends of a golden age.

Italian Wines

It is an interesting question why Italy, which produces more wine than any country in the world—even France*—should generally produce wine of inferior quality. No doubt soil and climate have something to do with it; the hottest countries do not produce the best wines, almost as if too much sunlight made the vines lazy. But the major reason is undoubtedly that it is only fairly recently that Italy has had much of an export trade in wine. A lot of wine was made; for Italy, as Cyrus Redding remarks, is one vast vineyard; but it went down the throats of the locals. This also meant that most peasant proprietors preferred grapes of high yield but low quality. Whether careful cultivation will ever create Italian wines to rival Romanée Conti and Château Margaux is anybody's guess. There is no sign of it yet.

It is understandable why Italian wine is not tremendously popular in England. You may buy a bottle labelled Chianti, in its straw basket (actually, all the best Chianti is exported in claret-type bottles), and you will probably pay more than a pound for it; the wine will be rather sharp, fine for washing down a meal, but with little or no bouquet; almost any bottle of ordinary Médoc is a better buy. Moreover, since Italy has no wine laws like France's *Appellation Contrôlée*, there is nothing to stop any Italian merchant putting anything he likes into a straw-covered bottle and calling it Chianti. The Americans, having a large Italian population, import a great deal of good

* France makes 1,332 million gallons (imperial), Italy, 1,455 million.

Chianti, although it tends to be pricey. The English import relatively little. So the best advice to an English wine-drinker is to avoid Chianti altogether, or use a reliable wine merchant where you are sure you are getting the real thing. Alternatively, buy some Italian wine whose label is less misleading: Barolo, Valpolicella, Bardolino, Barbaresco.

If you must drink Chianti, then it is best to begin by learning about it; I would suggest beginning with Luigi Barzini's delightful book *The Italians*. The chapter on 'The Power of the Family' contains some blood-curdling stories of adultery and revenge, which leads me to suspect that the Italians don't worry about the taste of their wine because they are too busy brooding on revenge and murder. There is a story (which has nothing to do with wine—but shall I not be allowed an occasional digression?) of the witty and good-natured Count Papadoli, who was aroused from his slumbers one night by the sound of heavy breathing under the bed, and realised that he had surprised one of his wife's lovers when he came in. In the morning, when the coffee arrived, he placed one cup on the floor, enquiring politely 'With sugar or without?'

But according to Barzini, Chianti also owes its existence to a husband's jealousy. Baron Bettino Ricasoli was a tall, cross-eyed man, who was Prime Minister of Italy for a short time in 1861. 'One night,' says Barzini, 'when he had been married only a few months, Bettino . . . took his young wife Anna Bonaccorsi to a ball in Florence. There the poor lady was briefly and perfunctorily courted by a young man, who danced with her a few times. The husband immediately told her: "We must leave, my dear." He escorted her to their waiting carriage, sat next to her, told the coachman: "To Brolio." Brolio was the family seat, a lonely and gloomy castle, lost in barren and sterile hills, where none of the Ricasoli had lived for ages. The couple rode in silence through the snow, until dawn, he in his black evening clothes, she shivering in her ball dress. They lived in Brolio for practically the rest of their lives.'

And to amuse himself, the 'iron baron' (as he was known) experimented with planting vines. The wine of the Chianti area was, at that time, as coarse and purgative as most Italian *vins paysans*; Ricasoli tried a mixture of black and white grapes—

Sangiovese, Black Canaiolo, Malvasia and Trebbiano, with seventy per cent of Sangiovese. Other wine-growers of the area began using the same methods—including an induced second fermentation by adding must from dried grapes—and the wine of Chianti (a district of Tuscany, in central Italy) began to acquire its present fame. Chianti, then, which is now almost a synonym for Italian wine, is a relative newcomer to the wine scene.

The best Chianti is from Brolio. The area which produces Chianti Classico covers about two hundred square miles of the Tuscan hills—roughly the same area as Beaujolais. The Italian government *is* strict about a wine label stating truthfully its area of origin (this is the meaning of the seal with the words *Italia Marchio Nazionale*—National Trademark), so a bottle of Chianti that says it is Classico or from Brolio is to be trusted. Other wines from outside this Classico area may call themselves Chianti, and their quality *may* be equal to that of the Classico—or it may not. All Classico Chiantis have a black cock on the neck of the bottle, and a number, indicating precisely what number bottle it is in that year's total output. Other genuine Chianti, from further afield, may have a pink cherub on the neck of the bottle. Chianti Rufina comes from the Florence area, and is rather heavier than most other Chiantis. This name—of a village—should not be confused with Ruffino, another reliable label (the name of a family), whose best Chianti is called Riserva Ducale. These both have the cherub (*putto*) neck label. The Melini Chiantis are made from Classico grapes, but outside the Classico area, so they use neither the black cock nor the cherub neck label; but they are of excellent quality; the best is Stravecchio Melini. Other remarkable Chiantis are the Brolio Riserva—the best of the Brolio Chiantis, Castello di Meleto—another Brolio—Antinori (a Classico) and Nipozzano, sold in a claret-shaped bottle, again with a cherub. The *fiaschi* (straw-covered round bottles) used to indicate that it was a Chianti intended to be drunk young, while the Chianti meant for ageing came in the claret bottles; this rule no longer applies invariably, but may be used as a guide.

The chief problem of writing about Italian wine is that it can be dealt with in two pages or two hundred, depending on how much space you have to spare. This does not apply to bordeaux, burgundy or hock, because there are important variations, and you cannot be brief. There are plenty of variations in Italian wines, but hardly important ones. And there are so many of them. I have Luigi Veronelli's book *The Wines of Italy* (1964), beautifully produced with pages of actual wine labels. But the section describing the wines occupies more than 200 pages, with about three wines to a page. Opening it casually, I find many wines that sound delightful; this, for example: 'Merlot Trentino. Suitable for ageing. Beautiful ruby red colour with orange reflections, pronounced bouquet of strawberries and raspberries. Dry taste, aromatic, completely harmonious. . . .' (Trentino is, of course, in the far north, adjoining Switzerland, so many of the wines sound as if they might be Swiss or German: Sylvaner, Traminer Aromatico, Küchelberg. . . .) To even list the wines Veronelli describes as superior or individual would take pages. But although most of them would probably taste agreeable enough with a good Italian meal in some small Italian town, they are hardly worth seeking out in London.

So let me compromise with a few generalities about Italian wine, and a mention of those most likely to be encountered abroad.

Much of the red wine has a light, clear colour, as if made with a mixture of red and white wine, and is light and easy to drink. Italy also has a wide range of white wines, some sweet, some dry, but many of these will strike the foreign palate as flabby and without character. This does not apply to Soave—meaning gentle—a dry, Chablis-type wine, regarded as the best wine of its type in Italy. Other reds are heavier in colour—notably Barolo, often regarded as Italy's greatest red wine, and sometimes likened to burgundy, although the Barolo I have tasted has been very light and clear. The wines of the far south also tend to be heavy and strongly flavoured—so that the Italians often drink them with fifty per cent water. Many of the white wines are sweet—these are usually made of Malvasia grapes; one of the best of these is Malvasia di Lipari, from Sicily, which has been described as smelling of broom, fennel, and liquorice. There are also various sweet red wines, notably the Aleatico family.

Anyone intending to sample a variety of Italian wines should memorise the name of the five major varieties of red grape, after which wines are named: Nebbiolo, Barbera, Dolcetto, Freisa and Grignolino. Many of the wine-names began with the name of the grape: hence Barbera d'Alba (a heavy red wine), Freisa di Chieri (light and dry, or sweetish), Nebbiolo d'Asti (a fizzy red wine I discovered in 1956, and consumed in quantity until I left London in 1957). Nebbiolo is the grape of Barolo and Gattinara, the two great reds; Barbera also produces a heavy-ish wine that tastes best after two or three years. Dolcetto, as the name might imply, is a light wine intended to be drunk young; this is also true of Grignolino. Freisa wine, as noted above, is sweetish.

Apart from Chianti, Italy's most popular wine abroad is Valpolicella, a wine of the Veneto in Northern Italy. I was introduced to it by the painter Pietro Annigoni, who turned up at my house one weekend with a crate of it. It was hot mid-summer weather; together with Bill Hopkins, we drove around Cornwall—which Annigoni had never seen—and occasionally opened a bottle of Valpolicella. I usually prefer to drink in the evening, sitting in an armchair; but I found that Valpolicella went down remarkably well on the beach opposite St Michael's Mount. It has the light, clear colour of a claret, and a slight flavour of bitter almonds; it can be drunk cool, and seems to quench the thirst more than most wines. It is closely related to Valpantena, so that I would not like to be asked to guess which of the two I was drinking—although Valpantena is supposed to be lighter in body. This is also true of the third member of the same group, Bardolino, which has been called Italy's Beaujolais, a very light, pink-ish wine with an aftertaste of sweetness. All three are made from Corvina, Negrara and Rossara grapes. For a long time, I kept a few bottles of Valpolicella around the house, and drank it when I felt like a light, clean wine. But I found that I missed the greater depth of French wines, even Beaujolais; subsequently I came across the Wine Society's Carafe, which invites drinking in the same casual, thirst-quenching way. Annigoni and I subsequently got through a fair amount of Valpolicella at his favourite club in Chelsea, when he pointed out that the virtue of the wine is that you *can* continue drinking it until the early hours of the morning, and wake up with a minimal hangover.

Also sold in flasks, like Chianti, are the white Orvietos; these may be sweet—the most popular—or dry; the latter is a new-ish innovation, in response to the taste for dry wine. Opinions on the dry wine differ; some say it is simply not Orvieto, others that, although inferior to the sweet, it is a delightful wine, with an acid after-taste. (Creighton Churchill says it has an after-taste of leather.)

Italy's other famous dry white wine is the romantically named Lachryma Christi, grown on the slopes of Vesuvius, and no doubt owing its peculiar quality to the volcanic soil. This quality has been described as flowery (elder flowers and broom) and also as scorched wine; otherwise the wine is not unlike certain dry hocks or wines of Bordeaux. There is also a sweet variety and a red one, neither as popular as the dry white. From the same area come the white wines labelled Capri, only a proportion of which are produced on the island. They are also pleasant light wines, without great distinction.

I have not yet mentioned the wine for which Italy is best known in England—with the possible exception of Chianti—Asti Spumante, a kind of sweet champagne made in the classic wine region, Piedmont. I personally find it undrinkable, but it is deservedly popular with women and children—or, for that matter, anyone not used to drinking wine, who feels that it ought to be sweet. It is not made by the usual champagne method, which involves secondary fermentation in the bottle. The Moscato grape, from which it is made, lacks staying power, so the makers of Asti Spumante—centred in Asti, Canelli and Allesandria—use a quicker method which involves making the wine in closed vats, then bottling under pressure. There is also a drier type called in Italy Gran Spumante, and sold abroad as champagne.

The sweet white wine that I find altogether more agreeable is Marsala; this is made in Sicily. It is a fortified wine of the port or sherry type, and in the nineteenth century, used to rival these in popularity. It was actually invented by two Englishmen, John and William Woodhouse, who visited Sicily in approximately 1760, and noted the high alcohol content of the wines around Marsala in western Sicily. It struck them that they might make a basis for a wine to rival port, sherry and Madeira, and to undercut them in price. I have already pointed out that the further south you go in Italy, the less delicate become the wines; in fact, most of the wines of Sicily are downright coarse and harsh. So the idea of disguising this by fortifying it with brandy was an excellent one. In 1773, the first shipload of Marsala sailed for England. But it was about a quarter of a century later that the wine experienced a sudden upsurge of popularity, as a result of the warm recommendations of Nelson, the national hero, who ordered a quantity for the Fleet at Malta, and remarked that Marsala was so good that any gentleman could allow it on his table. It was only in the present century, with the increasing taste for dry wine, that the English have ceased to be the best customers for Marsala.

Finally, I should mention vermouth, although this is not a specifically Italian product—it is also made in France and California. This is not a wine, but an aperitif based on white wine, flavoured with various herbs, including the flowers of the shrub *Artemisia absinthum*, whose leaves are used to make absinthe. Originally, the Italian vermouth was dark brown and sweet, and the French vermouth amber and dry; now both countries make both kinds. Cinzano also markets a colourless sweet vermouth—Cinzano bianco—which makes a superb long drink with plenty of ice and perhaps a little soda water. (I find it useful to offer to female guests who are unaccustomed to wine, but can't make up their minds what they want.) The attraction certainly lies in the clean, fresh taste given by the herbs—the same pleasure as smelling lavender or pine needles. In France and Italy, a vast quantity of white wine that would otherwise be fit only for local consumption is converted into vermouth, particularly the wine of hot regions, which tends to lack character.

If this were an encyclopedia, I would feel obligated to devote another long chapter to the wines of the rest of the world: Central Europe, Spain, Portugal, Austria, America, Australia, South Africa. It would bore me, but I would sigh and get on with it. Indeed, when I first began reading books on wine—a delightful occupation for winter evenings—I often felt irritated that their eminent authors wrote as though France and Germany were the only two wine-producing countries of the world. I have a curiosity about wines I have never tasted—I have rather the same feeling about music, which leads me to buy records by composers I've never heard of, simply in the hope of finding good music that is ignored in the concert halls. And with the music, at least, I have been very lucky; I have piano concertos by middle-Europeans whose names defy pronouncing and some of them deserve to be heard at least half as often as the Grieg and Schumann and Rachmaninov second. My curiosity about wine has been less rewarding; for although I have come across many pleasant wines from the Balkans, Alsace, California, none of them was more than mildly interesting. My friend Malcolm Rayment, the composer and music critic, suggested that I widen my acquaintance with the wines of Yugoslavia and Czechoslovakia, on the grounds that they are cheaper than French or German wines of comparable quality. The East London wine firm of Teltscher Brothers sent me two 'test cases' (if I may be forgiven the pun) of reds, whites and rosés, with names like Kavadarka, Cviček, Stanusina, Dingač. Most of them had a pleasant, light quality; I became particularly fond of the Kavadarka (which is the name of a grape), a light-ish red wine with a faint touch of almonds—it could quite easily be drunk cold, like a white. And the prices are, on the whole, lower than those of French or German wines. Yet after a few months of constantly drinking these wines, I found that my palate tired of them, in a way it has never tired of Beaujolais or Moselle.

One's response to a wine depends to a large extent upon the circumstances. In illustration of which, I may cite the case of an American wine that I encountered in Bozeman, Montana. I was staying at a pleasant hotel in a main street that was somehow permeated with a feeling of the old Wild West. It was certainly cow country; the steaks had to be seen and tasted to be believed—half the size of the plate, and deliciously tender. I asked if they had a red wine to go with it. They had no wine list, but someone was despatched to the cellar to see what they had. He returned in five minutes with a bottle of port. I explained this wasn't the kind of red wine I meant, and suggested that I go and take a look in the cellar. He took me down, and I had a chance to see for myself that there was nothing resembling what *I* meant by a red wine—not even a bottle of New York burgundy. And then, as I was about to leave, I noticed a few burgundy-shaped bottles in a corner of a shelf. The bottle had a label with a picture of a monk, and was labelled Christian Brothers Burgundy. The barman hazarded the opinion that it was probably an altar wine, and I was inclined to agree; still, I decided to try it. To my surprise, it was excellent; I was so pleasantly surprised that I finished the bottle and ordered another. And for the rest of my stay there, I drank a bottle every day. When I got back home, I looked up Christian Brothers in William Massee's *Wines and Spirits*, and learned that they are one of the largest and best wine-producers of the Napa Valley, California's main wine-producing region; their wines, he says, are generally soft, and without much character, but are often better than the acid *vins ordinaires* you drink in France.

A year later, living in Virginia, I asked the local wine store to get me a crate of Christian Brothers burgundy. It was rather more expensive than I had remembered—perhaps because it had to travel two thousand miles—and I now found it disappointing. I had been hoping to find an American wine as good, for everyday drinking purposes, as the cheaper French wines at three or four dollars a bottle. The Christian Brothers wine *was* a good wine for everyday drinking, and considerably cheaper than the cheapest French wine; but whenever it came to the point of choosing between Christian Brothers and a $4 Beaujolais, my hand strayed to the Beaujolais—simply because it had an additional depth and character.

Spain

I spent most of the autumn months of 1969 in Deya, Majorca; I was supposed to be a kind of Writer in Residence at an American College—Dowling—that had opened a branch there. My acquaintance with Spanish wine had been limited to bottles labelled Spanish Burgundy, drunk at parties—the kind of wine referred to as plonk, meaning that all that can be said for it is that it is red and alcoholic. I usually found this palatable enough, but with an after-taste that reminds me of nettles.

At our local grocer in Deya, the wine was sold from barrels—red and white—and you paid a few pence deposit for the gallon jar. It was sweetish and very cheap—the equivalent of ten pence a gallon, and, as you would expect at that price, had no more distinction than a gallon of cold tea. I occasionally drank quantities of it late at night, at students' parties, but could never bring myself to drink it in my own home (that is to say, in the house we rented). There were better wines, sold in bottles simply as red or white, and these I found suitable for everyday drinking, although still with too much sweetness for my taste.

The good wines, in restaurants, were from the Rioja, in northern Spain; the climate there is cooler, the grape season shorter, and the character of the wines resembles that of the wines of France. The most expensive wines on the wine list were those of Marqués de Riscal and Marqués de Murrieta, which are generally acknowledged to be the two best of the region. They certainly had character and subtlety, but I felt they were over-priced. (This, of course, may have been the fault of the Spanish restaurants.) This did not prevent me from drinking them whenever I could afford it. Marqués de Riscal struck me as having a claret-like quality, a lightness and elegance, but without any of the subtler qualities of good claret. It was a relief to drink them among the sweetish wines of Majorca, but I would not go out of my way to find a bottle in England. I tasted one Majorcan wine that seemed to me to compare in quality with the two Marquéses. This was at dinner with Robert Graves, and Graves's wife Beryl told me she bought it direct from the vineyard in Valdemosa, the next village down the road (where Chopin spent a miserable winter with Georges Sand). Perhaps I overestimated its quality, after drinking the local wines purchased from the local grocer, but it seemed to me to have the quality of a good but ordinary Bordeaux.

The only other Spanish wine I tried in Majorca was Valdepeñas, a sort of Spanish Beaujolais from La Mancha. Raymond Postgate had remarked that the wines of this region have a 'clean and almost stony taste which, if developed, could produce a great wine'. I found it robust, a little acidy, but agreeable, and

I would have drunk more of it if it had been more available in Deya.

It remains to add that Hugh Johnson has stated it as his opinion that the wines of the Rioja are the best value in the world today—that while the best old Reservas compare favourably with fine French wines, the ordinary cheap red is actually superior to French *ordinaire*. And my friend George Rainbird, in his book on Spanish wine, states that he has never yet tasted a bad Spanish wine. On the evidence of these two authorities, I am willing to accept that the wines of Spain deserve closer investigation.

Portugal

This may also apply to the wines of Portugal, although I am somehow inclined to doubt it. Warner Allen devotes most of his book on the wines of Portugal to port and Madeira—both are discussed elsewhere in this book. On the few occasions when I have tasted Portuguese wine, it struck me as good, but not outstanding; reasonably priced, but not cheap.

The wines of Portugal are classified as mature (*maduros*) and young (*verde*); either of them may be red, white or pink. The green wines can certainly be delicious in Portugal—fresh, crisp, slightly fizzy (or crackling), like a young Moselle—the wine Miss Laski thought might be John Keats's claret. But I have not seen this on English wine lists. As might be expected from its character, it comes from the north. The *maduros* wines from further south are less popular than the green wines; they are usually big and full-bodied, and, perhaps in the future, some Portuguese equivalent of Baron Ricasoli or the Marqués de Riscal might produce the equivalent of a good Hermitage or Châteauneuf-du-Pape.

The only widely-known Portuguese wine in England—apart from port—is the pink *vinho verde* known as Mateus rosé, which is the most popular pink wine in England or America. (The Americans pronounce it M'toose.) I find it too sweet—if I feel like a pink wine, I prefer a medium dry Anjou, or even a Bordeaux rosé; but its popularity is understandable. The music critic Burnett James once came near to causing serious damage to his whole family when he made the mistake of opening a bottle of Mateus with a gas corkscrew, which scattered the bottle to the four corners of the room—fortunately missing the children.

I am told by South African friends that their red wines are very good, but if I have ever tried any, I no longer remember the occasion. South Africa is a hot country, and the wines of hot countries tend to be strong but to lack finesse. Besides, the South Africans themselves are spirit drinkers—they like the hard stuff. I am told that they think nothing of driving a couple of hundred miles for a party, and certainly the few South Africans I have known have shown remarkable stamina in the art of celebrating and generally living it up. Much of their wine is distilled into brandy; much is fortified and turned into sherry. So there seems to be, at present, no reason why they should try to produce wines to rival those of France or Germany. But according to André Simon, in his article in *Wines of the World*, the quality is improving. Harry Waugh, reporting on a visit to Cape vineyards in 1962, spoke of several red wines as pleasant, and pointed out that they cost less than two shillings a bottle in their country of origin. He also commented that the white wines tended to lack bouquet and the fruity acidity of the best German wines, while the rosés were too heavy and too sweet to be refreshing. The country clearly has the resources for the production of good wine, but the interest is still lacking; the majority are not even sold with a vintage year on the label.

When I first came to London, at the age of twenty, I occasionally drank a bottle of Australian burgundy, sold in a *bocksbeutel*-type flask, and found that it produced the required effect—of mild intoxication. A Frenchman who lived in the next room always drank it, and said that it compared well enough with French *vin ordinaire*. I have occasionally tried it since, but never with pleasure. When you taste a wine, the first impression is the actual taste on the tongue, which is followed instantly by the real flavour, the bouquet; finally, after you have swallowed it, there comes the after-taste. In French wine, the flavour stage is usually distinctive—even if harsh. In the Australian burgundies I tried, there was very little of this developed flavour. The first taste on the tongue was velvety, slightly sweet, followed by a muted, heavy flavour, followed by some slight after-taste not usually associated with wine, like the foxy flavour of some New York wines. A few years ago, I noted that the Wine Society was listing an Australian wine called Malbec at about ten shillings a bottle; and since you can hardly go wrong at that price, I ordered half a dozen. It was, as the catalogue said, a sound wine of burgundy character, well worth the price, but totally and thoroughly ordinary. Such a wine makes one realise what one takes for granted in French wines. If I play a gramophone record with the bass and treble filters turned down as far as possible, I get a muted, dull sound, a lack of the distinctive shimmer of strings and the resonance of brass. This is how Malbec struck me, a wine without top or bottom. Vyvyan Holland has described drinking a wine from Mount Pleasant, in the Hunter River district of New South Wales, which was so like a Pomerol—a Château Petrus at that—that he suspected his host of trying to trick him. No doubt there must be many such in Australia; but no wine merchant seems to think it worth his while to ship them. I *have* tasted excellent Australian white wines—for example, a Barossa Riesling, which tasted not unlike an Italian Soave, with a touch of an Alsatian Riquewihr —an altogether more distinguished wine than any Australian red I have tasted.

Of the major wine areas of the world, there are only two on which I have anything still to say: Greece and Hungary; or, to be more specific, retsina and Tokay.

Retsina is, as every wine writer explains, an acquired taste; but it is not difficult to acquire it. I did so in 1960. I can be specific about the date, because it was the year of the publication of my first novel, and the book provided the excuse for a dinner party at which I first tasted retsina. I was collaborating, at the time, on *An Encyclopedia of Murder* with Pat Pitman, the wife of the *Express* journalist, Robert Pitman; and both were among the guests. The party was at a hotel in Surrey, and I left the choice of food to the Greek proprietor, a renowned cook. When I arrived at the hotel, I asked him what he intended to give us; he laughed and said: 'A thirty-course Greek meal.'

Assuming he was joking, I also laughed. The dishes began to arrive, on plates the size of ashtrays—garlicky-tasting substances wrapped in vine leaves, small cubes of mutton served with sliced banana, chopped aubergines with olives and sour cream, mussels stuffed with onion, a paste made of fish eggs. . . . At first I thought these were hors-d'oeuvres, but after the ninth or tenth, it dawned on me that our host hadn't been joking about the thirty-course meal.

The wine looked like Chablis or Graves; it was in huge carafes. And it tasted exactly as a disinfectant smells. I thought it awful. This was, of course, retsina: wine which is given its peculiar flavour by the addition of resin from pine trees. (There is a belief among many retsina drinkers that the resin preserves the wine; this is untrue. More probably, the old Greek wine took its flavour from the wine skins, which had been cured with pine resin. Or perhaps the resin was added later, to disguise the taste of goat.) I went on drinking the stuff because there was nothing else to wash down the meal; and having eaten my way through as many of the thirty courses as I could manage, I found I had got used to it, and was rather enjoying it. The first mouthful is the worst. I asked the proprietor the name of the wine merchant, and ordered a couple of cases. It was very cheap—less than ten shillings a bottle. I soon discovered that if I started the evening with a glass of it, I had to go on drinking it; once the palate has adjusted, other wines taste insipid.

Bob Pitman died in 1968 of leukemia; whenever I taste retsina now, I recall him with affection; like most journalists, he preferred whisky or beer as an everyday drink; but we shared some good bottles of burgundy in restaurants.

Of Tokay, I also have an anecdote to tell. In 1956, Esmé Percy was acting in *Gigi*—the play, not the musical. Peter Hall was directing, and his wife, Leslie Caron, played Colette's *ingénue*. (Esmé had known Colette and her husband Willy in Paris; it was he who told me that Willy was a writer-*manqué*, who derived his satisfaction from playing Svengali to his wife.)

One evening, Esmé invited me and my wife to a late supper at his flat to meet the Halls. Earlier in the day I had been interviewed by an American magazine—it may have been

Time—and when I mentioned the supper, the interviewer asked me whether it might be possible to come along and take a photograph. I said I doubted it, but that he would have to check with Esmé. Apparently he did so, for when I arrived at Esmé's flat, he told me that a photographer would be arriving after the meal. And, as a special treat, Esmé had bought some bottles of sweet Tokay to drink with the sweet course. It had sentimental associations for him. It used to be the great wine of the old Austro-Hungarian Empire; the best Tokay, Tokay Essenz, was a kind of super-*trockenbeerenauslese*, made by allowing the over-ripe grapes to burst under their own weight, so the juice retained all its fine bouquet. The name occurs as a kind of magic invocation in the pages of Arthur Schnitzler and Ferenc Molnar. Franz-Joseph used to send it to Queen Victoria for Christmas. But under Communism, this aristocrat among wines has become rare. Still, many fine sweet Tokays are still available, and some dry ones (generally of poorer quality).

The Halls both looked tired—*Gigi* had only just opened, and the strain of production still showed. But during the meal they brightened and became livelier. At this point there was a knock on the door. 'That must be the photographer,' said Esmé, 'I've told him he can only stay five minutes . . .', and he went to open the door. Into the room trooped a whole camera crew, complete with arc lights, tripods, great coils of wire. . . . If Esmé was annoyed or taken aback, he did not show it; his politeness was always superb. For half an hour, while we ate, they clattered around us, and then turned on the arc lights, so we were bathed in a blinding brilliance—with the inevitable heat. We tried to ignore them; we ate our strawberries and drank the Tokay; but it was no atmosphere for enjoying a great wine. Finally, they took their photographs, from all angles, and everyone was so subdued that we sat patiently until they packed up their equipment and left. We all said complimentary things about Esmé's Tokay, but I suspect no one really appreciated it. . . . Oddly enough, what I remember most about the episode was everybody's patience, as if the cameramen were an act of God; even afterwards, no one made the kind of angry comments about the press that might have been expected.

*

Scraping the barrel of memory, I can only add that I have occasionally drunk Chinese and Japanese wines (always white and dry) in restaurants and found them interesting, like some minor Loire or Alsatian wine, but unmemorable. The truth is that the larger part of the world's wines are commonplace; they are simply an alcoholic liquid, with no depth, no bouquet, no distinction. In his early play *A Phoenix Too Frequent*, Christopher Fry catches the essence of wine, what the word means as a poetic symbol; the Ephesian widow Dynamene, starving herself to death in her husband's tomb, accepts a drink of wine from the soldier Tegeus:

DYNAMENE: How good it is,
How it sings to the throat, purling with summer.
TEGEUS: It has a twin nature, winter and warmth in one,
Moon and meadow. Do you agree?
DYNAMENE: Perfectly;
A cold bell sounding in a golden mouth.

But too few wines ever sound their bell in the mouth. Recently, on a brief trip to London, I drank some Médoc, Barolo, Bardolino, Beaune, Volnay (Les Caillerets), and a bottle labelled Bordeaux that was distinctly corked, but not enough to be undrinkable. The only 'cold bell' that sounded was in the Volnay, a '65, which I drank with friends—Dr Raymond Pietroni and his wife Jennifer; this had the typical fine, velvety flavour, the superb bouquet, and—I noticed it clearly in the first mouthful—a definite smell of violets. Both the Italian wines were very good—and rather expensive—but what this means mainly was that they had no negative qualities; they had perfect manners, but no virility. As to the Médoc, drunk with British Railways food, it was a perfectly adequate wine; indeed, more than adequate (it baffles me how it survives the jarring of the train, but it does). And it possessed a personality, a kind of grace, that was lacking in the Italian wines.

And so I conclude, with a certain unwillingness, that Saintsbury and Maurice Healy and Morton Shand and Alexis Lichine are right when they imply that the only wines worth knowing about are French and German. The wine lover who knows his burgundies and Bordeaux, with a smattering of information about the wines of the Rheingau and Moselle, knows as much about wines as is worth the trouble of remembering. The rest may be looked up in an encyclopedia—Lichine and Schoonmaker are the two best—as and when necessary.

A concluding word on the subject of port. I realise that, by slipping it in like this, as a kind of postscript, I may upset many of its devotees. Saintsbury, Healy and Alec Waugh allow it a chapter to itself. For all that, I have my suspicions that the age of port is past. I can understand why Saintsbury should have enjoyed his port with a dessert pear, and why Alec Waugh can say of tawny port that there is no wine which, with cheese and a slice of cake, better rounds off a lunch party; port *is*, somehow, a wine that makes one think of leisure and of the past. Peacock was fond of his port, and it seems perfectly right that Squire Headlong and the Reverend Dr Opimian should consume a couple of bottles after dinner, while they debate whether the world is progressing or deteriorating. And Mr Waugh points out that the twentieth chapter of *The Egoist*, by Peacock's son-in-law, contains one of the finest passages on port ever written; it seems right that Sir Willoughby Patterne should have been a devotee. But I am not. Whenever a bottle of Old Vintage or Cockburn's Director's Reserve arrives in one of those Wine Society Christmas cases—which I buy out of a childish pleasure in the lucky dip—it usually stays at the back of the spirit cupboard for six months or so, to be finally consumed by lady guests (with lemonade) or by the children. But this is a matter of habit rather than of any real likes or dislikes about port. There is no *time* when I feel like a glass of port. When I have eaten my dinner, I continue to drink red wine, and on the rare occasions when I feel self-indulgent enough to vary the routine—or when I wish to tempt a guest to be self-indulgent—then I take a brandy or a glass of Calvados.

I was not always so indifferent to port. As a child it was the only wine I had ever tasted, and I felt that it tasted exactly as wine *should* taste—rare, expensive and delicious. The very words 'port' and 'sherry' somehow tasted delicious. While I was still living in Notting Hill Gate in 1956, I discovered that the local Henekey's sold their own Old Tawny Port, and I consumed a fair quantity of it. But not at the end of meals. In the sheer delight of discovering how pleasant booze could be, I drank anything at any time. And even though I soon discovered that the best time to start drinking is around six in the evening, I had no hard and fast rule about what I drank then. It might be whisky or sherry or Cointreau or Tia Maria or Crème de Menthe—I particularly favoured a drink of Crème de Menthe and Vodka in equal proportions, which took away the sticky sweetness of the Crème de Menthe while leaving the peppermint flavour undiluted. If I drank the Henekey's Old Tawny, I poured a large wine glass full of it—for I liked to be able to taste it. I became rather hypercritical about port; I liked the burnt-caramelly, nutty flavour of good port, and the stuff sold as 'Ruby' struck me as little better than mouth-wash. Indeed, I can recall only one occasion when I drank the latter; it was at a Cider House in the Edgware Road, where Stuart Holroyd and I took Iris Murdoch for a drink one evening. The place has since disappeared; it was the kind of pub that was bound to disappear, being very scruffy, with plain wooden floor, drab brownish walls, and a smell of disinfected sawdust. Apart from cider it sold gin and whisky; and above the counter there was a handwritten notice advertising Ruby Wine at sixpence a glass. The person who introduced me to the pub told me this was a euphemism for a concoction that contained methylated spirit.

I think Iris found the place rather alarming. As early as nine in the evening it seemed to be full of drunken Irish navvies. One aggressive old lady with a leathery face staggered over to our table flourishing an umbella, and for a moment we thought she was going to be quarrelsome; but she was more interested in Stuart, who looked deceptively young and angelic. She prodded him between the legs with her umbrella and asked: 'Ish it a boy or a girl?' It was after this encounter, perhaps in relief that it had passed off so well, that I suggested we might try the methylated spirit. I bought three glasses of the Ruby Wine, but it proved to be completely insipid, with a smell like pear drops and a taste like sugared water. I drank it; but I needed a pint of rough cider to wash away the taste.

The grapes of the Douro, from which port is made, are so rich in sugar that they ferment too fast, and the result is a harsh, raw wine without staying power. Presumably one way of preventing this would be to cool down the fermentation process by refrigeration; but in the seventeenth century, the only way of slowing it down was to add brandy. Someone discovered that if rather a lot of brandy is added—a fifth—the fermentation becomes so slow that it takes years, but the end result is a wine of great richness and depth. Vintage port—port made in a year of particularly good wine—is matured in the bottle, and so is crusted port, which is made of blended wines of various years. Both these wines produce a crust, and need to be decanted very carefully indeed. Wood port, matured in a cask, is a less aristocratic drink; its varieties include the ruby port I have mentioned (although the stuff I drank in the Edgware Road was a port-type wine rather than a port), and white port, which is a pleasant aperitif. As ruby port ages, it becomes brown in colour; this is the tawny I used to drink in London; it is twelve years old and upwards, whereas ruby may be drunk at eight.

I have only once drunk old vintage port. In the early sixties, a neighbour of ours, Gillian Carlyon, inherited the family house, Tregrehen, near St Austell. (Her brother Tristan, a friend whose help I acknowledge in my novel *The World of Violence*, had died in a car accident in Africa.) Investigating the cellars, she came upon a quantity of vintage port that had been there since the late nineteenth century. Having no particular liking for the wine she decided to sell it; but she was also kind enough to give me a couple of bottles—warning me that, once it had been decanted, it had to be drunk immediately. We left it for a few days to allow it to settle—on its side, with the dusty half of the bottle uppermost, to simulate the conditions it had known in the cellar—then decanted it with enormous care. It was a magnificent wine, thinner and lighter than any port I had tasted, but so fragrant that it was almost enough to sit sniffing it. Bill Hopkins and my wife helped me drink the two bottles, in the course of the same evening. We left a small amount of the decanted wine in a tightly corked bottle, and tried it the next evening; but Gillian was right; it now tasted rusty and completely dead.

Gillian later told me how much the wine had fetched at auction; I can no longer recall the sum, but it was in excess of

£5 a bottle. And although I thought it a splendid wine, I remember thinking that no port is worth that much. Even in these days, a good vintage port can be had under £2 a bottle; was that stuff of the 1870s really worth nearly three times as much? I doubt it. The pleasure of drinking old wine lies at least fifty per cent in the imagination; although the enormous prices it commands are not as criminally absurd as those of original paintings. For when a Florida millionaire drinks a bottle of 1860 Château Latour for which he has paid $100, he is at least drinking something unique; an alchemist could labour for years and be unable to recreate it. The processes of modern art reproduction can manufacture copies of a Michelangelo that are totally indistinguishable from the original for £10 each; only an art expert could tell the difference. In that case, where is the justification for paying half a million pounds for the 'original'?

Even where wine is concerned, there is room for scepticism. In *Wine in Peace and War*, Evelyn Waugh describes an evening in the barracks at Chatham when he and a brother officer decided to sample the two varieties of port on the menu, one slightly more expensive than the other. Waugh could not detect the difference, but the other officer thought one was rounder. They carefully compared them, sipping first from one glass, then the other, until Waugh agreed that the more expensive one *was* subtly better. Having forgotten which was which, they called the Mess Corporal and asked to inspect the decanters—whereupon he admitted that there was no 'No. 2 Port' on the wine list that evening, and that they had been drinking from the same decanter.

My brother Barry told me that he had once been challenged to tell the difference between a glass of Guinness, a glass of beer and a glass of water. He was blindfolded and then handed each in succession. After that, he had no idea of the order in which the glasses would be handed to him; he says that after a dozen mouthfuls he had no idea whether he was drinking Guinness, beer or water, for the lingering taste of the last mouthful—and the one before that—disguised the taste of the next. I doubt whether Waugh would have been able to tell the difference between ruby port and old vintage if he tasted them one after the other, as he describes.

And, as a postscript to this postscript: a friend who recently visited Oxford confirms my suspicion that the age of port is past. The warden of his old college told him that they have a hundred or so cases of vintage port that is now past its peak; in a year or two, it will be undrinkable. And unless there is a revival of interest in port, the same fate awaits hundreds of other bottles that were carefully laid down nearly two decades ago. My friend asked why they didn't sell it, or even give it away, and was told that this would be against the college statutes. Saintsbury would have groaned at this ultimate proof of the decadence of his old university. . . .

FOUR

Beer and Spirits

OUR ANGLO-SAXON ancestors drank mead, a beverage made with fermented honey. I mention it at this point because for many years I assumed it to be some form of sweet beer, rather like Mackeson's Stout. In 1954, I was working as a clerk for the Victoria Wine Company in North Finchley; in my desk drawer I came across a pamphlet advertising mead. It was being manufactured at a village called Gulval, near Penzance in Cornwall. According to the brochure, the building used to be a monastery, and there was a delightful picture of a cool, stone-flagged courtyard. There are half a dozen varieties of mead, ranging from sweet to very dry, sold in tall hock bottles. Whereupon I decided that I would take a holiday in Cornwall that year, and taste the drink of the Anglo-Saxons. In late July, Joy and I set out hitch-hiking to Cornwall, having sent our bikes on ahead to Plymouth by train. It was my first visit to the county where I now live, and it made a tremendous impact on me; it was somehow amazing to realise that the scenery really *was* as beautiful as in photographs. But the visit to Gulval was a disappointment. The mead manufactory had closed down for lack of funds. (The building itself looked more like an old warehouse than a monastery.) A nearby pub had some bottles of mead on its shelf, but the proprietor said he wanted to keep them for show.

Three years later, when I had come to live in Cornwall, I finally managed to taste the Gulval mead; it was at Gurnard's Head, where I had gone to see the Scottish poet W. S. Graham, who then worked as a coastguard. The Gurnard's Head Hotel had some bottles of mead, and the owner was willing to open one of them for us. It was a curious drink, fairly dry, with a very faint smell of honey; I have since tasted hocks that reminded me of it—hocks with a yellowy colour and an odd flavour not unlike geraniums. It was not an immediately striking drink; yet I think that, given time, I could have become a devotee. The Gulval dream was a noble one: of reviving the old mead industry, and making England as famous for its meads as France or Germany for their wines. And why not, since bees need only flowers, and flowers flourish in climates far too cold for grapes? We might even discover that the honey from flowers grown in Edinburgh or Aberdeen produces a mead of peculiar depth and astringency, while the honeys of the Home Counties are the equivalent of the Gamay grape, producing plentiful but unexciting mead. . . . I hope that one day some eccentric millionaire will finance another Gulval project.

By way of postscript, I should add that I visited the Gulval monastery a year ago, having heard that it had now been turned into a pub. We got there shortly after opening time on a hot August day. The place still looked like an old warehouse. The door stood open, but there was no sign of a bar—only a long, cold, stone-flagged corridor that echoed our footsteps. There were great wooden chairs that looked as if they had been part of the furniture of a monastery. We found the bar at the end of the corridor. I asked for mead, and the barman took down a nip size bottle from the shelf behind him. I stopped him, for I had seen these before; they contain a brown, sweet sherry-like liquid. I asked if he had no mead in wine bottles; he said he thought he had, and vanished for a moment, reappearing with a larger bottle. The mead he poured was golden in colour, like a medium sherry, and smelt fairly strongly of honey; but I found it an insipid drink, less good than an average sherry. Clearly, the possibilities of English mead are still to be exploited. . . .

Recent developments in the manufacture of beer furnish another argument for an English mead industry. Not only has it become weaker—as a recent government report reveals—but also standardised.* If I had written this book twenty years ago,

* And this is largely because the water itself has become standardised. The old local beers owed their flavour to the water of the area—it might even be to a single well. Increased demand meant that these individual sources of supply became inadequate; firms of chemical consultants were called in to create an artificial version of the special water, or perhaps simply to treat all the water piped into the brewery so that it tastes the same.

it would have been worth my while to travel to different parts of England sampling the beer and observing local differences; now I would taste the same brews from Penzance to the Hebrides. At least half the draught beer is now sold in metal canisters instead of barrels, and driven out by gas. It looks good, being clear and sparkling; and publicans tell me it is easier to keep. On the whole, it probably tastes better than the brews of twenty years ago—for the publican who really cares about his beer has always been a rarity. But there is no longer that exciting possibility of stopping at a dingy village pub and tasting a beer of complete individuality.

I am not saying that all beer has become homogenised; only that individuality is rarer than it was. If I am in the Midlands, I drink Ind Coope and Allsop beer, or Mitchell and Butler's, and their draught is quite different from the Devenish I may drink in a Plymouth pub, or the BB and Extra made by our own local brewery at St Austell. In the Midlands and the North, mild beer is obtainable everywhere; here in the West Country it is seldom seen. Speaking from memory, I would say that Mitchell and Butler's mild ale struck me as strong and slightly sweetish; Devenish bitter has a sharper flavour, which seems to agree with the natives of Devon, who are also fond of rough cider. Our local St Austell Extra is a strong beer with more hop-smell than some of the northern beers; when I first moved into the area, I drank nothing else in pubs. But then, I seldom drank more than a couple of pints. When my parents moved in to live with us in 1959, I began to spend whole evenings in the Mevagissey pubs with my father; then I found it wiser to switch to the BB (best bitter—although the locals refer to it as boy's beer), which is less potent.

But all forms of modern draught beer whether strong or weak, mild or bitter, would have been classified by our ancestors as small beer. The wine experts who condescend to mention beer seldom have a good word to say for small beer; they point out that ordinary mild can be drunk after seven days, whereas good strong ale may be kept for seven years before it is bottled. This may be true; but a nip of barley wine (which is actually a beer) is as strong as a nip of whisky; it may even be stronger. As far as I am concerned, they act far too quickly. (I should mention that mild is only about 3 per cent alcohol, and bitter little over 3.5 per cent; bottled Worthington and Bass are 4.2 per cent; barley wine and such drinks are anything between 6 and 10 per cent.)

These strong ales have their place. On the trip to Cornwall I have already mentioned, we cycled back along the north coast, turning off at Hayle towards Hell's Mouth. We intended to stop for sandwiches and a beer in a pub, but as closing time approached, there was still no pub in sight. Then, with a quarter of an hour to spare, we sighted the pub at Gwithian. On the shelf behind the bar there were several bottles with a bright purple label which carried a coronet. This was the Coronation Ale, made for the coronation of Queen Elizabeth the year before. It must have been at least 6 per cent alcohol. With a plate of sandwiches, it was just what we needed; a strength restorer, the perfect relaxant. After two of these, we cycled on a few miles to Hell's Mouth, and I then slept in the sun for half an hour, soothed by the cry of sea birds and the noise of the waves.

Lecturing in Oslo in 1957, I also discovered the virtue of strong ale, which the Norwegians brew at Christmas and call Julöl (Yule-tide beer). Landing in Oslo from the mild, soft weather of Cornwall, the icy Norwegian air caught me by the throat; even after a week there, I failed to get used to this cold that struck you a blow in the face every time you ventured out of the warmth of the hotel. I understood why the Norwegians liked the Yule beer strong, and why the Scandinavians in general drink so much spirit. In that temperature, my Worthington 'M', delightful in Cornwall, would have tasted as mild as cold tea. I drank the dark brown Julöl, and was glad at the immediate warmth it produced.

In America, a beer called bock is made in the spring—purportedly from the sediment taken out of fermenting vats. This, like Julöl, is closer to the beer our ancestors drank. I must admit that, apart from bock, I found American beers very disappointing indeed, although their lightness makes them an agreeable drink on a hot day. Harold J. Grossman declares that the correct temperature for beer is 45° Fahrenheit, but in the stifling, almost equatorial heat of Virginia in midsummer, I found that the colder my canned beer, the better it tasted. On the whole,

I found the popular American beers unsatisfying, and took to buying bottles of imported Worthington and Guinness at inflated prices. The popular American beers are essentially lagers—which means a light, carbonated beer; but I found that, as soon as the thirst was quenched, they lacked the quality of European lager; sometimes I suspected that they were flavoured by soaking cardboard in the vat instead of hops. I found it easier to drink these beers in airport bars than at home, where they seemed somehow anticlimactic. On the other hand, some of the stronger canned ales were of a reasonable quality. On lecture trips to distant places, I always made a point of enquiring about the locally made beers, and in that way discovered a few excellent ones—unfortunately I long ago forgot the names.

A word about the processes which produce different varieties of beer. I have already mentioned that the first step is the malting of the barley—allowing it to germinate, to convert starch into sugar. After this it is roasted in a kiln. This roasting determines the colour of the beer; lightly roasted barley makes bitter beers; for stouts, such as Guinness or Mackesons, it is roasted almost black. It is ground to a powder and mixed with water. This wort is then boiled with hops and sugar, and after filtering, it is ready for the fermenting process. If the brewer is making ale, which is stronger than beer, he will increase the temperature of the fermentation; beer is made between 37 and 49 degrees Fahrenheit, ale between 50 and 70. The yeast also determines the difference between ale, beer and lager. Lager and beer yeast ferments at the bottom of the vat, ale yeast at the top. Beer fermentation takes from eight to eleven days, ale less than a week. Finally, the young beer is run into tanks to be stored at a low temperature, while the impurities settle; this takes six months or so. It is then ready for drinking—in the case of English draught beer—or for carbonating, in the case of bottled beer; the carbon dioxide released during fermentation is used for this purpose.

The quality of the beer depends on many factors, chief among them the water and yeast. In the days before chemical analysis of water allowed a certain control, the great beers came from places that happened to have water of the right composition—

Munich, Düsseldorf, Pilsen (in Czechoslovakia—the home of Pilsener). The colour of brown beers and stouts depends not only on how long the barley is roasted, but how long the wort is boiled, converting the solids to liquid.

What *is* a good beer? I was a beer drinker for years before I drank wine, but I could hardly tell whether I was drinking a good pint or not. On the radio the other day, I heard a group of young northerners who had made a tour of England's pubs, looking for good beer. Asked about his criteria, one of them said that a good beer is cool but not too cool, and that it hits the back of the throat like a short (i.e. like a glass of whisky). Thinking about this, I suppose these are the standards I would now apply. (Out of a hundred or so pubs, these northern investigators discovered only three where the beer was of superlative quality, one in Manchester, one in the Midlands, and one in Portsmouth.) But in my younger days, I usually drank beer to wash down lunchtime sandwiches, so all that mattered was that it tasted nutritious; for this reason, I preferred brown ales or sweet stout—Hammerton or Mackeson. I found Guinness—*pace* my old friend Jonathan Guinness—too bitter for me; but when in Dublin, I soon noticed that the Irish Guinness seems to have a gentler quality. A pub on the Liffey, near the O'Connell bridge, produced us ham sandwiches and draught Guinness that I still recall.

I am no longer a beer drinker, for two reasons. First, and most important, I found that long sessions at the General Wolfe and in other local pubs were causing an alarming increase in my weight. Throughout my teens and early twenties I had a lean and hungry look, and my weight never increased above eleven stone (154 lbs, for American readers). At about the age of thirty, I soared up to 14 stone (196 lbs), and showed no sign of stopping there. In Seattle, in 1967, I began to diet determinedly, eating a single egg with a buttered biscuit for breakfast, then nothing else all day until evening, when I allowed myself a can of beer, half a bottle of wine, and supper without potatoes. In two months, my weight slipped from 14 stones to 11½. I cannot claim that I felt any better, or even that I looked a lot thinner, but the scale showed the difference. In March 1968, we left Seattle to return to England. During the two years in America, I had accumulated an enormous amount of junk, including hundreds of books and records. I sent on most of the books by sea mail—in forty large parcels—but if I had sent the records in the same way, the Customs would have charged me duty (a completely iniquitous procedure where gramophone records are concerned; why can we not treat them, like books, as cultural necessities?). So we had to return by sea instead of air. And if we wanted a private lavatory, we had to travel first class. (Since I treat the lavatory as a place of meditation and spiritual refreshment, this was a necessity.) The food and wine in the first-class dining-room were so good that it seemed a pity to continue to diet—in fact, a shameful waste of money. So I gave up the struggle, and took full advantage of three magnificent meals a day. Oddly enough, in the four weeks at sea, I gained only about 8 lbs, so I didn't feel too badly about the self-indulgence.

I have still to come to my second reason for giving up beer; that a couple of pints in a pub in the early evening (when I do my occasional pub drinking) spoils the taste of wine when I get home. So now when I go to the local for an early drink and to gossip with friends, I drink half a bottle of wine, usually Moselle. Besides, I find it easier to stop after half a bottle of wine than after three half-pints of beer, the legal limit for drinking and driving. I calculate that half a bottle of wine, which is about 10 per cent alcohol, is the equivalent of a pint and a half of beer, which is about 4 per cent. A half bottle of wine seems a satisfying amount to drink early in the evening, whereas I find it very difficult to resist the temptation to have another half of beer.

Saintsbury has an amusing story about the mixing of beer and wine. He and a friend visited a rose grower somewhere outside London, and ate an enormous lunch with beer—'some of the best draught Bass that I remember'. After this, their host produced a bottle of Chambertin. Now nothing would tempt me to drink Chambertin on top of large quantities of beer—it would be an infallible recipe for a bad hangover—but Saintsbury and his friend risked it. And since it was a warm summer afternoon, they decided to walk the ten or twelve miles back to London. 'I remember that for the first part of the way I felt as if there was a thin India-rubber or air cushion beneath the soles of my boots.' But by London, they were sober again.

With regard to hangovers, I have a curious and interesting discovery to relate, and I suggest that readers should test this for themselves. A few years ago, after a long evening of talking and drinking with guests, I went to bed feeling distinctly drunk; as I closed my eyes, the bed seemed to rock around me and my stomach turned somersaults. I had a hard day's writing in front of me next day, to meet a deadline, and the thought of my stupidity in inviting a hangover so annoyed me that I decided to get up and walk it off. Accordingly, I dressed, and walked down to the beach—it was a windy night. Half an hour later, when I climbed into bed, I felt better, and the hangover in the morning was mild.

The next time I went to bed with the consciousness of having drunk too much, I decided to do it again. And, in fact, I had roused myself and prepared to get up when my wife came to bed; at this point, I changed my mind and went to sleep. In the morning, I observed that the hangover was mild, and went off after breakfast. The suspicion entered my head that it was not the walk to the beach that cleared my system, but that initial act of deciding to get up and walk it off. After all, half an hour's walk to the beach does not really burn up an evening's alcohol intake. I tried testing this hypothesis. The next time I went to bed after too much wine (I should emphasise that this is a rarity; left to myself I seldom go beyond a bottle), I tried 'selling myself the confidence trick', and convincing myself that I meant to go for a walk. However, I didn't *mean* it, and the next morning, I had a bad hangover. Since then, I have discovered that the trick is to either go for a walk, or to *thoroughly intend to.* If I really intend to, it seems to work. I infer from this that the act of will sets some physical process going—analogous to our ability to wake up at a certain time—and this continues to work unconsciously in the night.

Whisky, brandy and other spirits

I have never been a dedicated whisky drinker—wine drinkers seldom are—but there have been periods when I've consumed my share. For some reason, whisky always tastes better in Scotland on a chilly autumn day. And when I first started drinking in Cornish pubs, most of my friends were whisky drinkers. I often joined them, and the taste of whisky immediately brings back those early days in Cornwall. I once quoted Charles Jackson's *The Lost Weekend* to Leonard Hibbs—the comment that it was not the whisky the hero liked so much as what it did to him. Leonard immediately contradicted this; he said that what he liked about whisky—and what, he believed, most whisky drinkers like—is the taste, that smoky, almost tobacco-ish taste. I think I understand what he means; when I have not tasted whisky for a long time, and I pour myself a small one in the early evening, I find myself thinking: 'Ah, I'd forgotten what a delightful drink this is.' But on the whole, I am suspicious of it. So many of the whisky drinkers I have known have been bottle-a-day men, and so many of them are dead. (Although I hasten to add that I have also met whisky drinkers in their eighties who seemed no worse for it; in Northampton in 1956, I met a man in his nineties who drank a bottle a day.)

I have met whisky drinkers who claimed that you can be a connoisseur of whisky just as of wine, and this sounds reasonable enough. Yet even here, I am inclined to doubt. When I first came to live in Cornwall in 1957, whisky was, for some reason, in short supply—perhaps it had something to do with the Suez crisis. Pubs often ran out of White Horse and Haig on the optic, and would suggest various less popular brands, including one manufactured by a West Country brewery. In the Commercial Inn at Roche one day, a car salesman of my acquaintance asserted that he would as soon drink paint thinners as this West Country whisky. I asked him what was the difference; he said he couldn't explain it, but that it was easy enough to tell by the taste. One or two other whisky drinkers who were present agreed with him. Whereupon I suggested that I should buy a glass of each whisky the landlord had behind the bar, and that my friend should then try them, and see if he could distinguish the paint thinners. He went off to the Gents while the whiskies were poured, and a couple of other contestants looked the other way. Then my friend returned to the room, picked up each glass, carefully sniffed them, and finally tasted each one. After some hesitation, he indicated a well-known proprietary brand, which he always drank. 'That's the West Country brew.' We had put them into different-shaped glasses to prevent any mix-up, but it took the assurances of myself, the landlord and several onlookers to convince him that he was wrong. Two others tried it, and the results were only slightly better; no one could actually distinguish one proprietary brand from another. And this is not remarkable, if, as I have already suggested, it is possible for a blindfolded man to fail to distinguish between Guinness, beer and water after several swallows.

I am not denying that different blends of whisky have different tastes, and that a man who habitually drank Johnny Walker would not know the difference if you gave him Haig or Ballantyne for his first drink of the day. But I doubt whether he would notice if you changed the brand after an hour or so.

Maurice Healy tells a couple of stories that demonstrate that even seasoned drinkers may be unable to tell whisky from brandy—how Monsieur Hennessey, of Cognac fame, was visiting Cork, and was offered a ten-year-old John Jameson's Whiskey as a liqueur; he guessed that it was a Grande Champagne Cognac. Healy says he has tried the same trick on his guests, and that they failed to detect the trick, although he himself recognised an old Irish whiskey which Ronald Avery—the Bristol wine merchant—offered to him as a brandy.

My problem, with whisky as with port, is that I can never think *when* to drink it. I occasionally pour myself a small measure of single malt at six in the evening; but unless I then allow at least an hour before I switch to red wine, I find that it spoils my palate. Alec Waugh says that he finds whisky a good nightcap, even on top of wine, but I would be reluctant to try the experiment. I *have* known people who could mix whisky and wine without ill-effect, but I am not among them. And general observation has confirmed for me the view that the grape and the grain take to quarrelling when they reach the stomach.

It *is* true, nevertheless, that there is almost as much to know about whiskies as about wine. I made this discovery on a trip to Scotland in about 1963. Although I had never met him, I decided to call on the poet Hugh McDiarmid at his home in Biggar. His entry in *Who's Who* stated that one of his hobbies was hating the English; but I had known two Scottish poets who knew him well—W. S. Graham and James Burns Singer—

and both had told me that he was an amiable man of wide culture.

We checked into a hotel in Biggar, a small Scottish town that reminded me of our local town St Austell (as it was before building-mania transformed it). McDiarmid was known locally as Mr Grieve, or 'the poet'; in spite of his celebrity, I got the impression that he was not lionised in Biggar; one man in the bar remarked that he had no time for him because he was a Communist. He was not on the phone, so it was impossible to find out whether a visit would be convenient. I took a bottle of whisky, and drove off to his cottage. This proved to be some distance outside the town, at the side of a long farm track that cuts off the main road to Edinburgh. His wife Valda let us in, without even bothering to ask him whether he felt like seeing visitors. He was sitting in front of the fire in his armchair—it was a chilly October day—and I was glad to see that he had a bottle of whisky on the table beside him. I produced my own offering, which he accepted amiably. 'But let's drink this first'—he indicated the already opened bottle. I accepted some of it, and asked if I could have water. 'Try it neat first.' I did; it seemed very good. He explained, 'That's a single malt'. I asked what that meant, and he then explained that every Highland distillery makes its own distinctive brand of whisky—from barley malt, of course.

These malt whiskies are the Scottish equivalent of Château-bottled wines. However, the English did not take to the heavy, smoky fluid. In 1830, someone invented a patent still that would produce grain spirits. (I am not sure why spirits made from corn, wheat, rye, etc., are called grain as if barley were not a grain.) These were altogether lighter in colour and quality. The mixture of this lighter spirit with the original malt whisky was altogether closer to the Englishman's taste. The Highlands stuck to their malt; the Lowlands distilled grain spirit, and bought up Highland breweries to get the malt whisky for the mixing. The Distillers Company Limited, founded by John Haig and a small group of Lowland brewers—including Johnnie Walker, Dewars, James Buchanan (of Black and White) and Mackie and Co. (of White Horse)—decided to persuade the late Victorians to try their new drink.

An amusing, but probably apocryphal, story tells how James Buchanan took a crowd of friends into one of London's best restaurants, ordered an expensive meal, then asked for a round of Buchanan's Whisky. When the waiter said they didn't have any, the party rose indignantly and stormed out. The next time they came in, Buchanan's Whisky was available. . . . .

In fact, the English did not become enthusiasts for Scotch whisky until the First World War, when their normal supply of French brandy, Holland gin, Jamaican rum and the rest were cut off by the German Navy. It was, of course, the first time this had happened since the time of Napoleon (and even then, the British Navy remained master of the high seas). So the British drank all the whisky Scotland could produce—and no doubt Ireland too—and when the war ended, the taste was so developed that whisky became the wine of England as well as of Scotland.

Which brings me back to Biggar, and Christopher Grieve's erudite discourse on malt. . . . During the course of the evening, the poet Norman McCaig dropped in, together with Grieve's son Michael, who was working for the *Scottish Daily Express* in Glasgow. When he heard that we intended to make for the Highlands the next day, he suggested that we meet him in a Glasgow pub for lunch, where we might also sample the malt. And so we did, presenting ourselves around one o'clock, and settling down immediately to the serious business of studying the colour and flavour of the various malts. There was The Glenlivet—the only malt which is always preceded by the definite article, like a title—the richest and heaviest of the malts; Glenfiddich, lighter in colour, with the same round, soft taste, and its own distinctive flavour; Glen Grant, the only malt whisky then generally available in English pubs, pale in colour, delicate in flavour, but, to my palate, sharper than Glenfiddich; Glen Mhor, a beautiful, gentle whisky, which is still one of my own favourites among the malts; and half a dozen others. I cannot pretend that I learned a great deal about malt on that occasion, for the tastes soon blurred on my palate; but it was a grounding for which I was grateful. Later that afternoon, after lunch, we set out to drive north; but by the time we had reached the southern end of Loch Lomond, I was so sleepy that we checked into a hotel. I spent the rest of that day and the night sleeping off my first lesson in the infinite variety of Scotch whisky.

A couple of days later I had reason to be grateful to McDiarmid and Michael Grieve. In Portree, in Skye, we ran into friends—a group that included the poet whom I mentioned in the Introduction. We were taken to visit every pub in Portree, and when I collapsed into bed at about 3 a.m., I had a suspicion that I would be suffering from a hangover for the next week. But I had stuck to the same drink all evening—the superb malt whisky manufactured on Skye called Talisker (which, it seems to be generally agreed, is among the great malts). The next morning, I woke up, as expected, with a feeling of severe enfeeblement. On the boat, I found a comfortable armchair, and lapsed into heavy slumber. An hour later, I woke up, and to my delight, the hangover had vanished; there was not a trace of it. This was the first time in my life that a hangover had disappeared within a few hours—they usually last out the day. It confirms me in my opinion that hangovers are not due to the actual alcohol consumed, but to the various impurities that get absorbed with it. The greater the mixture of drinks, the more complicated the impurities with which the system has to deal. Someone with whom I was discussing malt whisky the other evening remarked that the Scots recognise it as more dangerous stuff than cheap firewater, for the freedom from hangovers encourages the belief that even a full bottle is a moderate intake, and the ultimate devastation to the system may be immense.

It was either on this, or on a subsequent trip to Scotland, that I discovered the malt that I drink most frequently—Springbank, made in Campbeltown. I had lectured at St Andrews, and then spent several pleasant hours with my hosts of the Students' Union, drinking and talking. I told them about my discovery of malt whisky; the next morning, the group who came to see me off presented me with half a bottle of Springbank. (They explained, apologetically, that they were unable to get The Glenlivet from the local liquor shop.) In *The Occult* I have described how, soon after setting out from St Andrews, I began to experience a curious oppression. Half an hour later, Joy told me she had severe toothache; my sense of oppression lasted two days, until she had the tooth pulled out by a dentist in Kyle of Lochalsh; I am certain that my own low spirits were somehow picked up from her, telepathically. But on the Saturday afternoon when her toothache developed, I was grateful for the half bottle of Springbank. I found it milder and sweeter (if that is the word) than The Glenlivet—so mild, in fact, that my three-year-old daughter —who wanted to taste everything I ate or drank—took several large swallows of it from the bottle before I could stop her. (David Daiches, in his book on whisky, records that in the Highlands it was given to new-born babies.) We spent that evening in an uncomfortable Perth hotel, and the remainder of the bottle made the stay more tolerable; unfortunately the Springbank had no effect on the impacted wisdom tooth.

When I returned to Cornwall, I ordered some Springbank through my local pub—the Ship at Pentewan. It took months to arrive, and even then, the publican had to order a dozen. I bought three bottles for home consumption, and another bottle was kept behind the counter at the Ship. For a long time, I was the only one who drank it. Then a few locals became curious about it, and tried it. In a few weeks, it became so popular that it became necessary to keep a bottle on the optic, and the remainder of the dozen vanished fairly quickly.

For some odd reason, malt whisky suddenly caught on in England that year—1964; one of the colour supplements ran an article describing how it had suddenly become the fashionable drink in London clubs; this is simply one of those odd coincidences, for although I told many people about my discovery of malt whisky, I doubt whether I had anything to with the spread of its reputation in London.

Ever since then, I have made a point of trying different malts at every opportunity. The Glenlivet is magnificent, but rather too heavy for my taste. Glenfiddich—perhaps the most popular in England—is lighter, but has its own individual dry flavour, which I find less agreeable to the palate than that of Springbank. Glen Mhor is a beautiful, soft malt; I used to be able to buy it from the General Wolfe, which obtained its supplies through Harveys of Bristol, but I have not tasted any since Harry Bramble left the Wolfe in the late sixties. The Wine Society supplies an eighteen-year-old malt called Macallan, made in Rothes, and this certainly qualifies as one of the world's greatest malts; a whisky-drinking friend of mine said it was the best he had tasted in his life, and described it as pure nectar. Lord Douglas Gordon, who used to own the Rising Sun at Portmellon—close to Mevagissey—told me that his favourite malt was Glen Morangie, made in Tain. John Hosking, the landlord of the Ship at Pentewan, obligingly ordered some, and I found it as good as Douglas Gordon had claimed, but so close in general style to Springbank that there seemed no point in switching. Talisker is a fuller and richer style, closer to The Glenlivet, as are many of the malts from the west coast of Scotland.

Campbeltown, the home of Springbank, was one of the first—perhaps the first—place in Scotland to make whisky; the art, apparently, was introduced from Ireland. Both the Scots and the Irish have the two essentials for good whisky—soft water and peat (although most Irish distilleries use coal); the latter is particularly important, because it is the peat smoke that imparts the individual taste to whisky.

There is no reason why whisky should not have been discovered by the same alchemists who made brandy in the twelfth century. For it is basically a distillate of beer. The early processes of whisky-making are almost identical with those in beer-making. Barley is soaked in cold water, then allowed to sprout, then smoked (rather than roasted) in peat smoke; then it is ground up and mixed with hot water, producing mash. After several washings, only husks remain—used for animal feed; the wort which contains the essence of the malt is now cooled, and fermented with yeast. If hops were added as flavouring, the result would be beer. This beer is twice distilled, producing a liquid with about twenty per cent alcohol, and known as 'low wines'. Then further distillation and purification produces a spirit that is more than fifty per cent alcohol. Spring water is added to bring it to the required proofage, and then it is aged in old sherry casks for a minimum of seven or eight years.

The patent still, invented in 1826 by Robert Stein, and enormously improved in 1830 by Aeneas Coffey, was the invention that revolutionised whisky-making, since it could produce vast quantities of the raw grain spirit that is mixed with malt whisky to make the popular blends. The Coffey still consists of two immense copper columns, forty or fifty feet high. The mash is made from maize and unmalted barley, which is pulverised and cooked at 140 degrees Centigrade. The basic principle of the Coffey still is of fractional distillation—that is, based on the recognition that different alcohols distil out at different temperatures. Both columns of the still are divided into chambers by perforated copper plates. Hot steam is passed upwards through one of the columns—the analyser—while the beer (known as the wash) comes in at the top, and descends plate by plate. (Not through the holes in the plates—the rising steam prevents this—but through a pipe, which conducts it to the next chamber on its downward progress.) By the time it has reached the bottom, the alcohol is vaporised and mixed with the steam. It now passes into the next tower, the rectifier, for the cooling process. (An ingenious touch—the cooling is done by the cold wash that is being introduced by means of a coiled copper tube; so the cold wash condenses the alcoholic steam, and the steam heats the cold wash to prepare it for entering the analyser.) Whereas the alcoholic liquid descends through the analyser, its steam rises through the rectifier; as it does so, the impurities are distilled off, and only pure alcohol reaches the top, and is drawn off into stainless steel vessels. This is matured like malt whisky, although it takes less time; it is basically a kind of vodka-like liquid, which is then mixed with malt whisky to produce the famous proprietary blends.

Until a few years ago, all the Irish whiskeys were malts—made in a pot still; more recently, the Irish have taken to blending some of their whiskeys to produce a lighter quality. The flavour of Irish whiskey (the Irish, like the Americans and Canadians, spell their whiskey with an 'e') is less smokey than that of Scotch, because the barley malt is dried over coal instead of peat. I have known drinkers who swear by Irish whiskey, although in England it is definitely an acquired taste. In early 1957, Joy and I were on our way to Ireland from the West Country; we crossed from Ilfracombe to Swansea on the ferry. (I remember, a loudspeaker was playing the César Franck Symphony, and that main theme of the first movement always reminds me of the windy deck of the Swansea ferry.) In Swansea, we had several hours to wait for the night train, and I decided we would call on Kingsley Amis, whom we'd met in London; at that time, not long after the publication of his second novel, Amis was still teaching at Swansea University. I rang him and he told me to come over right away. We arrived to find Amis and his wife Hilly surrounded by bottles. It was Hilly's birthday; she was fond of liqueurs, and there was a whole row of them on the table. Joy drank cointreau—in fact, I seem to remember she drank several liqueurs; Amis himself was drinking Irish whiskey, which he offered to me, explaining that he thought that a good Irish was better than most Scotches. I drank mine—I think it was a Jameson's or Bushmill's—with a little water, and agreed that it was excellent, mellower than any Scotch I had tasted (bearing in mind that at this time I knew nothing of malts). When we left for the night train, I felt as though I were walking on a cushion of air. In Dublin, the next day, I tried a glass of the same whiskey as an appetiser before lunch, but was disappointed; it was the same brand as the one I'd drunk in Swansea, but it seemed to me less delicate. In various parts of Ireland, over the following two weeks, I discovered that Irish whiskey *can* be far better than the average Scotch, but that it is variable. The quality of a whisky depends on the stillman, who has to remove the first and last part of the distillate, known as foreshots and feints. I assume that when too much of these impurities remains, the result is that odd, almost petrolly flavour, which spoils the softness. I have not tasted Irish whiskey in years, but in the days when I was sampling it upon Amis's recommendation, I came to the conclusion that you can never tell whether you'll get a fine, delicate whiskey, or one that tastes as if someone had added a thimble-full of crude oil to the bottle.

What is Proof?

This is the point to say a word about proofage. The Americans have a beautifully simple system: the proof indicated on the bottle is exactly double the amount of pure alcohol in the drink, so 80 proof means forty per cent alcohol. I wish the British system was as simple, but instead we have an absurdly complicated method of working out proof. We rate a drink as under proof or over proof. A drink that was 100 under proof would contain no alcohol at all. The turning point—at which under proof becomes over proof, is slightly over fifty-seven per cent alcohol—that is, 114 proof under the American system. The only point at which British and American proof mean approximately the same is half-way down the table—American 53 proof equals British 53.6. *After* the British 'O' proof (fifty-seven per cent alcohol by volume), over proof begins, and the American 115 proof is the English .7 over proof. American 200 proof (that is, hundred per cent!) is British 75.1 over proof. A more stupidly complicated system was never devised, and it is to be hoped that now we are in the Common Market we shall either use the American system, or the continental Gay-Lussac system, which is the simplest of all—alcohol by percentage—so that when a bottle of Châteauneuf du Pape states that it contains 12.5 per cent alcohol, you know what it means without bothering about proofage.

Since whisky is basically distilled beer, it should be possible to manufacture it anywhere in the world; but for some unknown reason, this is not so. I have occasionally tasted Hungarian whisky, Japanese whisky, but although it was undoubtedly a spirit, I would certainly never have guessed that it bore any relation to the drink I know as whisky.* One of these days some brilliant chemist will determine precisely why only the Scots and the Irish seem to be able to make first-rate whisky, and he will deserve the Nobel Prize. We know that it has something to do with the pure, soft Highland water ('through peat, off granite'), and with Highland peat, but beyond that, we are in ignorance. Even the still itself may have something to do with it; William Massee tells a story of a battered old pot still in the Highlands that finally became unserviceable; so the owner had a new still fabricated with all the old dents and scratches; the

* A comment I must withdraw. Since writing these words I have sampled Japanese whisky, Suntory Royal, that tasted in every way like a good Scotch—not Malt, perhaps, but a first class blended. In this case, the Japanese seem to have solved the insoluble problem.

result was an identical whisky. This sounds absurd, but brewers vouch that the quality of a whisky may change completely when the still is replaced.

The assertion that only the Irish and Scots produce first-rate whisky may cause some patriotic indignation; for the Americans and Canadians certainly produce some fine whiskeys. The Americans set up the first distillery on Staten Island in 1640. But the drink they called whiskey was made from Indian corn, with an intermixture of rye (i.e. was almost straight grain spirit). Lichine makes the interesting suggestion that early American farmers often found it difficult to get their grain to market, over the bad roads; so when rain or other problems threatened the crop, they distilled it into whiskey, which was as saleable as grain. Bourbon was first produced in Georgetown, Kentucky, by a Baptist minister named Elijah Craig, and although the name was soon used by most of the breweries in Kentucky, and some outside, it still refers mainly to Kentucky whiskey. Straight Bourbon is the equivalent of malt whisky, although it is aged only two years in wood. Blended Straight Bourbon sounds a thoroughly Irish drink, but it actually means that it is a blend of straight Bourbons, not, as with blended Scotch or Irish, a mixture of malt and grain spirit. Rye whiskey, manufactured mostly in Pennsylvania and Maryland, is often blended with grain alcohol, producing blended rye; again, this is only aged for two years. I have tasted some fine American straight ryes and straight Bourbons, but although they were satisfying drinks, with that quality that in a wine is called breeding, they were always simpler drinks than a good malt whisky—that is, without the subtlety and depth. My investigation into American whiskies was fairly limited because I quickly discovered that some of them are, as far as I am concerned, completely undrinkable. On my first trip to New York, my publishers gave a party for me, and the main drink was a well-known brand of American whiskey. I tried it, and found it impossible to understand how anyone could drink the stuff; the flavour was distinctly bitter. But my editor said it tasted fine to him. I take it that Americans who have been drinking this particular whiskey since high-school days—convinced by the advertisements that it must be good—simply accept that whiskey should taste as if it has been blended with Campari or Angostura bitters.

Canadian whiskeys are notable for their lightness; most of them are blended. They call their whiskey rye, but this is confusing, for the American straight ryes are heavy, full-bodied whiskeys, closer to the heavier malts; in fact, Canadian rye is made from corn (maize), rye and barley, the corn giving the lightness. (Corn whiskey is the traditional bootleg liquor; when I was living in Virginia it was still made all over the backwoods, and no doubt still is; it was often almost as colourless as vodka—which explains why it is sometimes called White Lightning.) In 1956, when I could first afford to keep a bottle of whisky in my cupboard, I soon discovered that I preferred the light—and slightly sweet—flavour of Canadian Club, although I also kept a bottle of Scotch for guests; what I liked about it was the exact opposite of the quality I found so disagreeable in the American whiskey I have mentioned. It does not possess the subtlety of a light malt like Springbank or Glen Morangie, but I have often found it a very acceptable alternative. If a comparison were to be drawn between whisky and wine, then I would say that the Scotches are the equivalent of burgundies, the Irish whiskeys of claret, while Canadian rye is roughly the equivalent of the wines of northern Italy—the Barolos and Bardolinos and Valpolicellas—light, distinguished, easy to drink. In this comparison, I am not sure where I would place the American whiskeys, although the wines of Spain might make a passable comparison: that is, often of high quality, but never as interesting as burgundy.

Before concluding these remarks on whisky, I should add that the most delightful book on the subject is Alfred Barnard's *Whisky Distilleries of the United Kingdom*, first published in 1887 by Harper's Weekly Gazette, presumably in instalments.* Barnard actually travelled to see all the distilleries of Scotland and Ireland, and the result is a kind of travel book that now induces a powerful nostalgia.

Of other spirits, I have less to say. I don't suppose I've tasted rum or gin in ten years. When I first moved to Cornwall, I

* Reprinted, 1969, by David and Charles.

discovered that gin and lime makes a very pleasant appetiser at six in the evening. The flavour of neat gin—English gin—always strikes me as somewhat disagreeable, like taking medicine; I could certainly never drink it neat, or with water. On the other hand, the charm of gin lies in that sharp, astringent flavour, which is so perfectly offset by orange juice or lime juice, or by that curious quinine preparation called tonic water. I feel that gin and lime is one of the most fragrant drinks I know—I much prefer its smell to that of whisky or rum. The fact that my use of the word fragrant will cause some raised eyebrows is a measure of how far we have allowed ourselves to become prejudiced by the mythology of Gin*—thoughts of Hogarth's Gin Lane with its prostitutes and footpads. The word wine has magic; so has brandy; gin is blunt and ugly.

Gin is basically grain spirit, although theoretically it could be made from pure medical alcohol. It is produced in much the same way as grain whisky or vodka—by distilling a kind of beer. After being distilled to a pure state, it is then re-distilled with various ingredients, principally juniper berries (juniper is called in Dutch *geneva*—hence gin). Other ingredients may include caraway, coriander, aniseed, cassia bark and liquorice, depending on the brewer's own formula. No ageing is required. Most of the writers on spirits claim to prefer Dutch gin to the English variety, but I suspect this may be snobbery. The Dutch drink their gin on its own, like vodka or aquavit; some of it certainly tastes completely unlike the English gins, which taste better with flavouring. Whenever I hear a mention of Dutch gin, I am reminded of an amusing story concerning Dan Farson. One evening in a London pub, Dan encountered a literary critic noted for his meanness. They reached the bar at the same time, and, after an awkward pause, the critic said: 'Let's have a Dutch drink'—meaning: Let us each pay for our own. Dan pretended to misunderstand him. 'Why, that's most kind. I'd love a Bols Gin.' The critic was so horrified that he stammered: 'No, I really meant . . .', and at this point noticed Dan's ironical smile. He blushed, bowed to the inevitable, and paid.

*

* 'London gin has a strong scent—like a rather vulgar woman's perfume, to be truthful.'—Raymond Postgate, *The Plain Man's Guide to Wine*.

Rum is a by-product of sugar manufacture. When the sugar has been crystallised from the heavy syrup, a percentage remains behind in the molasses. This molasses is fermented with yeast, then distilled. In the heavier Jamaica rums, burnt ale—the left-overs from the sugar vats—is added, and fermentation is allowed to proceed naturally. Caramel is usually added to darken the colour—rum may otherwise be as colourless as vodka. Storage in oak casks may also darken the colour. The most popular rum used to be heavy and dark—perhaps because this was the type used by the Navy; but in recent years, tastes have changed; light, golden-coloured rums or the colourless Bacardis are preferred.

I started my adult life with a prejudice against rum. When I was a small boy, at the beginning of the war, my father brought home one Christmas a bottle of a synthetic, non-alcoholic rum—presumably intended for flavouring trifles. I thought the taste delightful, and drank most of it—after which I was sick for hours. Even now, the smell of rum brings back a faint memory of that unpleasant Christmas night.

The prejudice vanished in Hamburg in the winter of 1957. I flew there after lecturing in Norway, intending to spend an evening with Bill Hopkins—who had gone there to write a novel that was to be set in Hamburg—and return to London the following day. It was a freezing December evening; Joy, Bill and I made our way to a bar in the Stefansplatz, and Bill suggested that we should warm ourselves with hot rum grog—that is, a long drink made of rum, boiling water, sugar and lemon juice. The stuff tasted so delicious in that climate that I ended by drinking half a dozen; by which time the bar seemed so charming that I decided to stay on in Hamburg for a few more weeks. Which we did, and made a habit of combating the cold with hot rum grog. Any bar would provide it; many of them even kept a kettle steaming on a low gas. I found it far and away the pleasantest pub drink (for, as I have noted, drinks in pubs taste somehow different from drinks at home) that I had ever tasted, and I would have continued to drink it after returning to England, except that publicans made such a face when I asked for it. I regard it as the best of all drinks for a cold winter evening.

Like gin—and unlike whisky or brandy—rum is a drink that needs to be flavoured. At least, this is my own opinion; it is not shared by most Cornish fishermen, who often (when the catch is good) drink neat rums between pints of beer.

I have drunk neat rum on only one occasion. When I first moved to Cornwall, I often drove to Leicester, my home town, to bring my parents down for a holiday. It is a long drive, particularly in midsummer, when the roads are crowded, and I usually found that it took me about forty-eight hours to recover. One August, we decided to try to avoid the heavy traffic by setting out late—about six in the evening. By ten-thirty, we had only got as far as Bath, less than half-way. At this point, we decided to stop for a pint of beer. It was near closing time—no time to drink a second pint; but I purchased half a bottle of rum—the thick, dark kind. An hour later, when I began to feel tired, I opened the bottle and swallowed a mouthful; my father also took a drink from the bottle. For the next half hour or so, I felt refreshed and relaxed. The roads were empty; the night was cool; periodically, my father handed me the bottle, and I took another mouthful. When we reached Launceston, about forty miles from home, I discovered the bottle was empty, and I was now drowsy. So I handed the driving over to Joy, and fell asleep in the passenger seat. I had never known a drive to pass so quickly and pleasantly. I had no sensation of being drunk—only a feeling of lightness and relaxation. But the state of my head when I woke up the next morning left me in no doubt that I *had* been drunk. . . .

'There is good brandy,' says George Saintsbury, 'and there is, though it is almost a contradiction in terms, bad brandy.' Saintsbury was, of course, one of the great *bons viveurs*; he cared for little else besides literature and good food and drink; in his later years, he gave his students the impression that he was wandering around in a dream. One of them, A. S. Neill, the headmaster of Summerhill, told me a typical story. Neill was editor of the university magazine, and was gathering material for the obituary of a professor who had recently died. He approached Saintsbury for his comments. 'As a matter of fact,' said Saintsbury, 'I'm just about to make some remarks about him to my honours class. If you're very quiet, you can come and sit at the back and take notes.' Neill said, with mild exasperation: 'But sir, I've been in your honours class for the past year.' (There were only a dozen people in it.) 'Oh really?' said Saintsbury, 'What's your name?' 'Neill.' 'Neill!' said Saintsbury, with surprise, 'How you've grown!' (Neill had been over six feet tall for many years.)

But to return to Saintsbury on brandy; he records that for several years he drank Australian brandy as an economy measure. And this, it seems to me, is the sign of a truly dedicated brandy drinker: that he should swallow an inferior variety because he likes the stuff so much. I have nothing against brandy, but I seldom drink it because I can never think of the right time for it. The logical time is after a meal; but, as I've already commented, I prefer to carry on with wine, and I find that brandy ruins my palate and makes the wine taste insipid. I occasionally drink brandy after a meal in a restaurant, to keep my host (or guest) company, and to enliven my sense of the occasion. In Majorca I drank the Spanish Fundador brandy; but this was because most of the wine was so awful that I needed a change. At home, the same bottle of brandy may stand untouched in the drink cupboard from one Christmas to the next.

When Saintsbury said there is good and bad brandy, he was thinking mainly of the vintage stuff. Nowadays, if you buy a bottle of Hennessey's XO or Martell Cordon Bleu or Rémy Martin, you know that you are getting a brandy of high standard; but it is a blend of brandies. The purpose of the blending is to make sure that any bottle of Cordon Bleu, bought anywhere from Hong Kong to Aberdeen, tastes the same. Brewers use the same argument about beer; and as smaller breweries are absorbed into larger groups, the local differences vanish. The result may be a good beer—sparkling, clear, light—but it is always the same.

In Saintsbury's day—or Maurice Healy's—you asked your wine merchant what he had to recommend, and he replied: 'Well, let me see. I have a very good but rather expensive 1889 Cognac from the vineyard of M. Picard, near Saintes. But I can offer you a fine 1908 from the vineyard of M. Dadier, outside

Jarnac, at about half the price. And I can also offer you an excellent 1902 Armagnac from the Laval Brothers in the Gers Department at just over two pounds the bottle. . . .' It is still, of course, possible to get these vintage brandies, either from a good wine merchant, or direct from the grower; but it becomes increasingly difficult. And in the past year or so, even the good blended brandies have become preposterously expensive.

The two varieties I have mentioned above—Cognac and Armagnac—are reckoned to be the finest brandies in the world, Cognac leading by a short head. (Armagnac is drier.) The town of Cognac is in the Department of Charente, named after its river; on the map you will find it immediately to the north of Bordeaux. Landes, Gers and Lot-et-Garonne, the Departments that produce Armagnac, are to the south and south-east. Some centuries ago, the natives of these areas discovered that their wines tasted poor and sharp compared to those of their neighbours of the Gironde; then someone tried distilling this harsh wine, and found that it produced a superb brandy. Like sherry or whisky, brandy is aged in casks—usually of Limousin oak; it differs from wine in that once it is bottled, it ceases to change—except, perhaps, to grow weaker. The finest Cognacs are grown near the town of Cognac, and are known (in order of merit) as grande champagne, petite champagne and borderies. Cognacs called *bois*—fins bois, bons bois, bois eloignés, bois communes—are from further to the east and are less fine than the *champagnes*, but still very good indeed.

Such brandies are, of course, intended to be drunk as liqueurs; it would be *lèse-majesté* to put soda or ginger ale in them. And beyond all doubt, they are the world's greatest liqueurs; you could rhapsodise about the depths and subtleties of a good brandy; it can evoke the ghosts of Christmas Past better than the spirits in *A Christmas Carol*; it has all that richness of mince pies, Christmas puddings and iced cake without necessarily being sweet or rich in itself; you might almost say they were for smelling rather than drinking.* There

* There is an amusing story told of Talleyrand. He offered a visitor a glass of brandy; the visitor gulped it down and replaced the glass on the table. 'That is no way to drink a superb Cognac,' said Talleyrand. 'I'm sorry,' said the visitor, 'how should one drink it?' 'First you hold the glass

are, of course, blended brandies that are both sweet and rich—Hennessey's XO is one of the finest. I recently had occasion to compare it with a Rémy Martin grande champagne, and it was like comparing a Richebourg with a Château Margaux; the XO was robust and magnificent, the champagne was subtle, like a rainbow seen through a shower. Both are too sweet for my palate; on the whole, I prefer the drier Armagnac, or a straightforward Calvados, the Normandy apple brandy. If I have spent an evening talking and playing records with a guest, I find a small quantity of Calvados the ideal night-cap; its smell is evocative of orchards on a cool autumn day, and the dryness refreshes and cleans the palate.

A few words about the labelling of brandy. Most of the best-known manufacturers now use the three star symbol to indicate their ordinary blend—what some drinkers refer to as cooking brandy. This is young brandy—it could have been in cask as little as three years. It should be light in colour, and it should *taste* light and clean. It should not be fiery or sweet. It can be an excellent drink—on the level, say, of a vodka or schnapps—intended to produce a warm glow rather than caress the palate and stir the imagination. There are many people who dislike the rather harsh, smoky aroma of whisky; brandy, with its touch of sweetness and its grapey smell, seems somehow more civilised. But I have noticed an interesting thing: people who drink brandy and soda are either less serious drinkers or more serious drinkers than people who drink whisky and soda. Many young men drink brandy because it tastes nicer than whisky; but, if their tastes run to spirits, they usually pass on to whisky. When a hardened whisky drinker changes to brandy and soda, it is usually the beginning of the end. I have seen it happen several times: when a man gets into the habit of taking too much whisky, and his doctor warns him that a few more thorough booze-ups will probably kill him, he stops drinking for a token period, then switches to brandy, as if to try and deceive his liver. I am no medical man, so I cannot speak about the metabolic

---

between the palms of both hands and warm it gently. Then raise it to your nose and sniff it.' 'And then,' said the visitor, 'you sip it slowly?' 'No,' said Talleyrand, 'you put it down and talk about it.'

effect of this change; but I have noticed, on two or three occasions, that the switch seemed to hasten the collapse. Perhaps the moral is to keep on corroding your system with the poison it has become accustomed to.

To return to grades of brandy: one stage above three star there is the grade V.O. (very old) or V.S.O. (very superior old) —these both indicate brandies between ten and twenty years old. V.S.O.P. (very superior old pale) may be up to twenty-five years old, while V.V.S.O.P. (very, very superior, etc.) may be forty years old. These initials are a generally agreed code among the major shipping houses—Martell, Hennessey, Hine, Bisquit, Rémy-Martin, Courvoisier, Otard, etc., but there may be divergencies: many of them start with V.S.O.P. as their lowest grade of liqueur brandy, and it might, on some occasions, mean between twelve and seventeen years old; so the letters must only be taken as a rough guide.

Finally I should mention *marc*, the *eau de vie* which is distilled from the grape pulp (or *pomace*) left behind when all the wine juice has been squeezed out. This is often fairly rough—it takes at least twelve years before it starts to become smoother, and the French peasants who consume it in large quantities are seldom willing to wait that long. (Gaston Dominici, the Provençal farmer who was convicted of murdering the Drummond family, was reported by journalists to drink at least two bottles a day.) It tastes grapey and leathery, and is something of an acquired taste.

Although it is a spirit, and most spirits will keep for years, brandy shares with wine a tendency to go off if exposed to air: it loses savour and pungency. I have always taken this to be an argument that, in spite of its alcoholic strength, in which no biological organism could survive, brandy is nevertheless in some sense alive.

To end this chapter, a note on vodka. The vodka that is drunk by the characters of Gogol and Pushkin was probably distilled from potatoes. Nowadays, most vodka is made from barley and other grains, so that the formula is basically the same as for whisky or gin; it would not be too inaccurate to call it unflavoured gin. The Russians drink it neat, like schnapps. In a

Leningrad restaurant I asked for two vodkas as an aperitif before the meal, and we were presented with two carafes, each holding about three-quarters of a pint. I have never attended one of those Russian dinners where endless toasts are drunk; but my wife has, and she tells me that the quantity consumed was incredible. I can quite believe this. A friend of ours settled down with, and eventually married, a White Russian exile, and became accustomed to drinking vodka. Staying with us in our cottage in Cornwall in 1957, she said that her Boris thought nothing of knocking back vodka by the half pint. I said that no one could drink a half pint of vodka without falling asleep ten minutes later. She disagreed, and offered to demonstrate. So I carefully filled a half-pint tumbler with 80 proof Smirnoff vodka —which is manufactured in Camden Town, but from a Russian recipe—and handed it to her. She drank it down almost without pausing, and I watched with fascination, waiting for her to collapse on the carpet. She didn't, and an hour later, she was still showing no sign of heavy intoxication—a slight gaiety, and an occasional stumbling over words, but nothing worse.

Russian vodka has a distinct oily flavour, but most of the varieties manufactured in England and America are practically flavourless. There *is* a slight flavour, which reminds me of the smell of acetone (used in model-aircraft cement), but it is hardly detectable.

I suspect that the popularity of vodka is due to the name: that is, to the same kind of cultural snobbery that makes the French so fond of whisky. James Bond's preference for vodka is a sign of his international know-how, like his knowledge of skiing and skin diving and foreign cities. In fact, vodka is a singularly unexciting drink; its chief use in England is to add an alcoholic content to tomato juice or orange juice. You cannot sip it, like good whisky or brandy. On the other hand, it has many negative virtues: the lack of smell and its chemical purity, which means that its hangover is less paralysing than those of other spirits. And on one occasion, I even used it medicinally. In 1958, I tried to revive a dying fire with what I thought to be paraffin; in my haste I had picked up a five-gallon drum containing petrol. The explosion blew me across the room, shattering my glasses, burning off some of my hair, and taking some skin off the back of my hand and one side of my face. The burn was extremely painful; but when I had gulped down about half a pint of neat vodka, it seemed less troublesome. I fortified myself with vodka for the rest of the day, and had a good night's sleep; the next morning, the pain of the burns had vanished. I had no noticeable hangover. I suspect that a similar quantity of whisky or brandy would have anaesthetised the pain but left me with a hangover to contend with.

FIVE

In Praise of Pubs

IT IS AN interesting reflection that membership of the Common Market may influence British drinking habits as radically as Henry Plantagenet's marriage to Eleanor of Aquitaine in 1152. And one that, in me, arouses a mixed reaction. The English pub is a curious institution, quite unlike the French bar or the German beerhouse. On the Continent, drinking is usually associated with eating. In England, there are still thousands of pubs where they regard it as an insult if you ask for a sandwich. Most ordinary locals still cater for the man who comes home from work, has his tea (he had his dinner at midday), then goes out for a couple of hours for a pint and a game of darts. If he feels hungry, he has to make do with a packet of potato crisps or salted peanuts. When I was a boy, some of the Leicester pubs also sold cow heels, pigs' trotters (both eaten with vinegar) and a very pleasant and filling substance called scratchings, which seemed to be made of small, hard fragments of pork which crunched between the teeth. But this was only on special occasions: in honour of visiting dart teams, or on Bank Holidays.

No, I suspect the Englishman regards his pub as the equivalent of the tribal council chamber; eating there would somehow reduce its status. The pub is a place for ritual drinking, 'buying drinks by rota', as they say in *Peter Grimes*.

I have never found out how this came about. But I have a theory. In France or Italy, there is no need for a pub on the English model. Almost every village makes its own wine and marc: they may as well drink at home. Most Englishmen do not brew their own beer; and even if they did, beer is not the kind of thing you can drink regularly at home. There is too much of it in a pint. A man who sits reading a book or watching television wants to sip, not take huge swallows. In a pub, it's different. The drink punctuates the talk; if there is a lull in the conversation, you can take a long, thoughtful pull at your beer. I have been in country locals where there were whole minutes of silence, broken only by the click of the dominoes. Except for the atmosphere of relaxation, you might have thought you were in church. And after ten minutes of this, the mind slips into a lower gear; time ceases to be important; you are contented just to sit there, and listen to someone's account of how he kept the birds away from his strawberries, or got rid of moles from his lawn. You may only stay for half an hour, but when you leave, you feel as relaxed as if you'd been away for a holiday.

Now I have no doubt that this also happens in French and German bars. But the English have a temperament for ritual; it explains our addiction to oratorios like Handel's *Messiah*—so puzzling to foreign musicians, who prefer their music to be symphonic or operatic. The pub routine becomes ritualised; you might say it becomes a source of psychological comfort and security. How otherwise can I explain why my father, when he is on holiday in Cornwall, dislikes moving from pub to pub? He says it is a waste of good drinking time; but this cannot be true, because he may sit for an hour with the same pint in front of him. The real reason, I suspect, is that he feels that movement from pub to pub indicates an attitude of frivolity towards the drinking ritual. A churchgoer would feel the same about visiting several churches on a Sunday morning and staying ten minutes in each.

I say this without irony. There is more in common between the church and the pub than at first meets the eye. As a child, I could never understand why people went to church; I could not believe they enjoyed it. When I came to live in the country, I began to understand. If you went to church throughout your childhood, it becomes a source of comfort, a link with your past. And for people living in villages or small country towns, it may also be an important part of the social routine, producing that warm feeling of belonging to a community. The village pub does the same—and it is also open seven days a week, and sells a beverage that helps to induce the feelings of wellbeing.

I had my first experience of the pub ritual when I moved to Cornwall in 1957. At that time, St Austell—our local town—still had a market day every Friday; that is to say, the pubs were allowed to stay open from eleven o'clock in the morning until closing time at night. In fact, markets had not been held in St Austell for several decades. In the mid-sixties, the local police pointed this out to the magistrates—to the fury of the locals—and we lost our market days. I still feel this was an unnecessary piece of legalism, for there was no drunkenness to justify the suspension. (I half suspect that the publicans were relieved not to stay open.) It is true that anyone who wants to drink all day can still visit Lostwithiel on a Tuesday, or Truro on a Wednesday, or Wadebridge on a Thursday—in fact, I believe that while St Austell still had its market day, it was possible for really devoted drinkers to spend every afternoon of the week in a pub by driving a few miles to a town that had a market day.

While we still had our market day, I made a habit of going into St Austell on Fridays; not because I wanted to drink all afternoon, but because I was sure to meet a crowd of friends in the back room of the General Wolfe, on the corner of the Bodmin Road. Joy went off to do the shopping, returning occasionally to deposit a bag of groceries under my seat. I ate bread and cheese and pickles, or a hot Cornish pasty, and drank half pints of Worthington 'M', a medium strength bitter which the landlord, Harry Bramble, kept admirably. (It was drawn from a barrel, not a canister.)

It never failed to astonish me how quickly and pleasantly those Friday afternoons drifted by. I have always been an obsessive worker; I dislike holidays, and am always glad to get back to my typewriter. But sitting in the back room of the Wolfe, I could understand how alcoholics could have 'lost weekends', or even lost months. Time ceased to matter. I left because Joy got tired of waiting for me, or because I became drowsy after my ninth or tenth half-pint—not because I felt any desire to get up and go. For apart from the almost Edwardian atmosphere of that small room, with its huge mahogany table, the company itself was exceptionally interesting. They were mostly farmers, businessmen, local traders, the occasional commercial traveller or bank manager. For someone like myself, a stranger in the district, they constituted an encyclopedia of local knowledge. They were also a glimpse into a way of life of which I—as a town-bred intellectual—knew nothing. It was like taking a time machine back to the England of my grandfather's childhood.

There was Dennis Watkins, the local land agent and auctioneer, who seemed to know every farmer and publican between Land's End and Tavistock, and the history of their families for generations. There was Bill Mallett, an ex-superintendent of the Cornish police, who could sometimes be persuaded to tell amazing and frequently improper stories about his days in the force. I have already mentioned Leonard Hibbs, who edited a national magazine, *Record Review*, from his office up the road, and who had in his home the best stereo sound system that I have ever heard. He had moved to Cornwall from London after the war, looking for a peaceful rural existence; but I sometimes feel he missed the pubs of Fleet Street. There was Leslie Evans, the optician, whose doctor had instructed him to give up whisky; so he drank Mateus rosé—always, I felt, with a wistful expression. And there was Buller Hawke, certainly one of the most remarkable and memorable characters I have ever met. Buller had a powerful stout body, a head that was almost perfectly globular, and a bass voice that made the glasses dance when he called for the landlady, or asked 'Who will take wine with Hawke?' Buller's real name was John Redvers Hawke —he was named after General Buller, from which I presume that he must have been born around the turn of the century. He had spent his youth travelling around the world as an engineer in tin mines—a 'Cousin Jack'—and now ran a fleet of lorries. The seat near the door was always reserved for Buller, for his sheer bulk made it necessary for him to be in a place where he could move out without disrupting the room.

Buller's birthday fell a week after mine; and from 1958 until the time of his death, we gave a joint birthday party in the back room of the Wolfe around July 1. This was a considerable saving for both of us. We provided a dozen bottles of champagne—Heidsieck—and our landlady covered the table top with plates of sandwiches, cocktail snacks, sausages and pasties; when the dozen bottles of champagne had been emptied, it was the custom for other members of the group to provide a bottle each. We started at lunchtime on Friday. Those who had work to do in the afternoon had to be strong-minded enough to tear themselves away after a couple of glasses. Towards four o'clock, Buller had tired of champagne; and since he could not switch to his usual drink, whisky, he would start to drink brandy. I stuck to champagne, for I was usually by this time close to my limit. Towards half past five, when the other pubs opened, Buller stood up, his face shiny but otherwise showing no sign of having tasted alcohol, and proposed that the company should move elsewhere. It had become a habit on his birthday to complete the day at the pub at St Stephens. I never went there with him—making it my excuse that they would probably have no champagne; the truth is that I would have been hung over for a week if I'd gone with Buller. He would stay out until closing time, drive home (I think his car knew the way, like an old horse), and then, like Socrates, be up the next morning as fresh as ever. On the rare occasions when he exceeded his proper limit, and woke up with a dry tongue, his wife Nell placed in front of him an enormous Cornish breakfast that included eggs, bacon, sausages, and sometimes liver and steak too. He admitted that he ate it to prove to Nell that he never felt less hung-over in his life; but he said it always had the effect of making him feel splendid an hour or so later.

Once a year—in January—Buller 'de-coked'—that is, he gave up drinking and smoking for precisely one month. He never experienced the slightest difficulty in doing this, or, as far as I know, any withdrawal symptoms. At the end of the month he would reappear in the Wolfe, looking—to my eyes—as healthy and vital as ever, and feeling, he assured us, ten times better. (Leonard Hibbs showed a similar strength of mind; one day in the back room, when someone challenged him to give up cigarettes—he smoked forty a day—he stubbed out the one he was smoking, and gave them up for two years. Then, having proved his point, he started again.)

Buller represented the old Cornwall—the Cornwall described so superbly by A. L. Rowse in his autobiographical books and poems. When he was forced out of business by a larger contractor, I felt that he lost some of the Rabelaisian vitality that made him seem larger than life; the booming laugh remained, and the deep voice asking 'Who will take wine with Hawke?', but I detected an underlying sense of having come to an end.

His considerable bulk placed a strain on his heart, and whisky did nothing to improve his blood pressure. His doctor warned him that if he wanted to live another ten years, he should lead a less hectic life. Buller, I am told, enquired thoughtfully how long he would have to live if he carried on as usual.

I had the dubious distinction of taking him on his last visit to his old haunts. One Tuesday lunchtime, I was in St Austell with Pat Murphy, an American Professor of Philosophy from North Carolina. We met Buller, and he suggested we join him for a drink in the Conservative Club. He began to talk about old times and old friends; then it struck him that Pat ought to meet some of the old friends. He asked us to pick him up at eleven o'clock the next morning; we would go to Newquay, to see a friend who ran a hotel there, and then on to Truro, where it was market day.

I went with certain misgivings, knowing that Buller's capacity was considerably greater than my own, even when he was drinking large whiskies to my half pints of beer. But the lunchtime passed quietly enough. We went to Newquay, met his friend in the almost empty bar of an enormous hotel, and sat there quietly until closing time, listening to their reminiscences. Then we drove to a place on a cliff top, overlooking the sea; Buller produced a large box, and from several layers of cloth, unwrapped hot pasties provided by Nell. By the time we had finished eating, I felt as sober as ever. But it was only the beginning. We drove to Truro, and (as far as I can remember) visited every pub in the place. Buller was everywhere greeted with shouts of welcome. By half past five, my first wind had gone, and my second; I had lost count of the number of half pints I had swallowed, or how often I had been to the lavatory. At all events, I resisted the temptation to reduce my liquid intake by changing to whisky. At about six, I suggested that we should start moving back towards St Austell. En route, Buller recollected more old friends in Probus, Grampound and Sticker. Finally, at about half past seven, we delivered him back safe to Mrs Hawke, declined the invitation to come in for a drink, and drove back home. Buller looked tired, but I have never seen him more cheerful. But he stayed in bed the following morning and, a few weeks later, died in hospital.

All this probably makes it sound as though Cornish market days are an excuse for drunkenness. This is untrue. There is heavy drinking, but I have seen very little drunkenness. There seems to be a different attitude towards drinking in the country, as compared to the town. I am thinking of, in my teens, cycling back across Leicester at eleven o'clock on a Saturday night, and hearing drunken men and women singing in chorus on the corner of Charles Street. The pace of life in a city adds a desperation to the heavy drinking, and there is something unpleasant and alarming in the spectacle, as if it is balanced on the edge of violence. I have never encountered this in the country; the pub is simply a pleasant alternative to an evening at home, not an escape. The same applies to the countryman's attitude to sport—Rugby football, soccer and so on; there is an absence of the hysteria followed by vandalism that seems to characterise the towns. Marx would say that the alienation of the cities has not yet spread to the country.

This accounts for my nostalgia for the old General Wolfe. I say the old Wolfe because it has changed hands in recent years and been modernised, so that it now looks like a West End bar. The back room has been demolished to make way for a restaurant. During the whole time I frequented the back room, the Wolfe had no telephone; old mother Bramble declined to have one of those unpleasant, shrill devices in the house. While mother Bramble served the back room, women were not allowed in—except briefly, to leave shopping with their husbands. When I first went there, in 1957, this rule had been relaxed, for mother Bramble spent most of her time in her room upstairs. She emerged occasionally to serve us during our fortnightly dinner. This was a custom that had begun a year or two before I went in. One lunchtime, a bank manager had commented that he had never tasted caviare. Leslie Evans, the optician, immediately offered to send for a jar from Harrods, if the bank manager would supply a bottle of vodka to go with it. The following Thursday, the back-room regulars foregathered, and ate caviare on toast, accompanied by vodka. One of them commented that he thought caviare no better than the lumpfish roe that could be bought in the local grocer's, and offered to bring a jar the following Thursday; this was also consumed with vodka. At this point, someone became ambitious, and offered to bring in a suckling pig, if Jean Bramble would roast it; this necessitated changing the meeting to the evening. When I joined, the twenty or so members each provided a dinner in rotation; the meetings took place throughout the winter, once a fortnight. But members no longer brought their own food to be cooked. The days when someone brought a giant hog's pudding, eight feet long, or Dennis Hocking, the county pathologist, was asked as a guest of honour to carve an enormous goose, were long past. We told Jean what we wanted to provide, and paid her for it afterwards. In summer it might be a salmon—probably poached in the River Fowey; in winter, a joint of salt beef with pickled cabbage. They were amusingly conservative about food. Colin Milton, who had spent years in Malaya before the British were thrown out, managed to persuade them to eat a mild curry with Bombay duck and popadams; but when I offered to provide a meal of grouse or pheasant, I was told emphatically that no Cornishman would dream of eating a bird that had been hung for a fortnight. We had roast beef instead.

Although no male chauvinist, I can understand mother Bramble's objection to women in the back room—or indeed, in pubs in general. At the end of the Victorian age, there was a reaction against their unrealistic view of women: the angel in the house, whose days are devoted to her home and children, who submits to sexual intercourse with the resignation of an obedient wife but never enjoys it, and who looks so demure that you would imagine she was 'solid from the waist down', as Joad once expressed it. Only fallen women drank and smoked and wore make-up. In the twenties they went to the other extreme. Women sometimes referred to themselves as chaps (as Lady Brett does in Hemingway's *The Sun Also Rises*). They wore make-up because 'all women want to make the best of themselves'. They smoked and drank because there were no longer taboos about it. They flirted because it was now acknowledged that women can enjoy sex as much as men. (But the idea was still piquant and slightly shocking; the Starr Faithfull case caused so much excitement because the dead girl actually pursued men.) But I am inclined to feel that this Roaring Twenties view of woman's nature was no more accurate than that of the Naughty Nineties; in fact, rather less so. Women are not natural pub-drinkers; at the point where a man is just beginning to enjoy a conversation about cabbages or boats, they get bored. They find the pace too slow. It is true that in cities women get into the pub habit; but that is largely out of lack of anything else to do. They sit at the side of their husbands and sip at milk stout or Advocaat and exchange gossip with somebody else's wife but the pub is simply a pleasant change from home—they might as well be at a sewing circle or jumble sale.

No, the real female pub-drinker seems to have a peculiar attitude to her husband, a kind of jealousy, a determination to be fully acknowledged by his friends. One professional man who came to a Wolfe dinner as a guest, and was subsequently invited to join, had to excuse himself because his wife had put her foot down; she usually went out drinking with him, and saw no reason why he should spend an evening in all-male company. And he was weak enough to allow her to dictate. Which brings me to another observation: the female pub-regular is often more dominant than her husband. After drinking too much, she may even drop hints that he is inadequate in bed. And such women *are* inclined to drink too much, and to become flirtatious as they become tipsy. If the selected male fails to respond, perhaps embarrassed by the presence of the husband, they may become aggressive. In many cases (and I am surprised how many I can call to mind) they have been very pretty women; but alcohol is unkind to the figure and to the complexion. Such women often make me think of Shaw's description of Mrs George in *Getting Married*: 'Her beauty is wrecked, like an ageless landscape ravaged by long and fierce war.' They often give the impression that they have missed the great love of their life, and are still hoping he might appear—perhaps this accounts for the liking for pubs. (It has often struck me that most of the women involved in murder cases are of this type: Ruth Ellis, Edith Thompson, Alma Rattenbury, Florence Maybrick, Madeleine Smith. . . .) If they finally lose this sense of deserving male admiration—and it often seems to survive in the face of all reason—they usually develop into full-fledged alcoholics.

All of which, I feel, explains mother Bramble's determination to keep her back room for men only. I am not saying she was wholly right. I often took women—guests who were staying with us—into the back room; the regulars obviously enjoyed it, and responded by putting themselves out to be friendly and entertaining; but this is because it was a break in the routine, not an everyday event.

I would not like anyone to conclude that I feel nothing but nostalgia about the Cornwall I knew when I first came here, twenty years ago. The St Austell of that time was a drowsy little town, with hardly a modern building in it; now it has a multi-storey car park and blocks of high-rise flats. But from the housewife's point of view, the supermarket is a distinct improvement on some of the old grocer's shops. And although it was more quiet and picturesque in the days before the invasion of the motor car, it must have been a great deal less sanitary. Mother Bramble once told me how, thirty or forty years ago, she could look out of the window of the Wolfe at night and see large rats strolling along the pavement. And it was only about twenty years ago that the local baker climbed into his van one winter morning, and was suddenly attacked by rats, who clambered over his head and shoulders as he started the engine—making, of course, for the open window. The top of his bald head was badly clawed by them. I myself have seen a huge grey rat waddling along the street in Fowey on a quiet summer evening, looking as casual and unconcerned as a dog out for a stroll.

No, I have no strong regrets about the old Cornwall, with its ugly houses resembling miniature Wesleyan chapels, its damp cottages with musty Victorian furniture (uncomfortable sofas covered in green imitation velvet), its sewers that ran direct into the sea within twenty yards of a bathing beach. But I regret some of those quiet bars and back rooms in which I have drunk a contemplative half pint; not just the Wolfe, but the Fountain and the King's Arms in Mevagissey, the Ship at Polmear, the Polgooth Inn (always cool on the hottest day), the Carlyon Arms at Sandy Bottom, the Commercial at Roche, and a dozen other country pubs between here and Penzance that have been 'converted' to attract the tourist trade. They may be more comfortable now; but they are unlikely to draw together a crowd like the regulars who met on Friday afternoons in the back room at the Wolfe. And *they* were the essence of Cornwall.

I have only one major criticism to make of my favourite books on wine—Saintsbury, Healy, Waugh et al. They are so concerned with the pleasant aspects of drinking that they ignore its darker side. In this, they reflect the attitude of our scientific age. The ancient Greeks knew nothing of the chemical composition of alcohol, or of its effect on the nervous system, but they recognised that there is something of a mystery about its effect on consciousness. A few glasses of wine can bring the glow of 'absurd' delight, the Proustian sense of ceasing to feel mediocre, accidental, mortal. A few glasses more can push the personality over some strange inner boundary, and place it at the mercy of its destructive forces, those forces the Greeks symbolised in Dionysus the avenger. This is the aspect of alcohol that fascinates me.

In May, 1942, a young American soldier stationed in Melbourne, Australia, asked his tent-mate whether he believed in stories of werewolves, and whether a real-life Jekyll and Hyde could exist. Edward Leonski was a gentle, good-natured character, noted for his enormous physical strength and for his placid, child-like character. But in two weeks, he murdered three women, with no apparent motive. Police found the third body lying naked in a trench half full of yellow mud near the army camp; they found the same yellow mud on the flap of Leonski's tent and on his bedstead. Leonski made no attempt to deny his guilt; if anything, he seemed relieved to be caught. He had been dropping hints that he was the killer ever since the first murder; but he was such a gentle personality that no one took him seriously.

As far as his friends were concerned, Leonski had only one drawback; whenever he drank heavily, he became aggressive and offered to fight anybody in the bar. This struck no one as very abnormal. But what they did not know was that if he went on drinking beyond a certain point, he became the victim of completely incomprehensible urges. After an evening spent drinking with a girl he had picked up, they walked home together, talking affectionately; she even sang to him. When she stopped singing, he had a sudden wild desire to 'keep her voice'. He attacked her violently, beat her to death, and ripped off her clothes. But there was no sexual motive; she would probably have been willing enough to take him home with her. He met his third victim, a middle-aged woman, when he was returning to camp after heavy drinking. He addressed her politely; they walked along, talking, until she turned to go. Then the impulse to 'keep her voice' came over him again, and he killed her and tore off her clothes. Psychologists found him sane, and he was executed. In my own view, he was not sane. His remarks about Jekyll and Hyde suggest that he found the destructive impulse incomprehensible; it was like a beast that lay in wait for him; and alcohol provided its opportunity to attack. Whether Leonski suffered from an Oedipus complex or a love-hate relation with his mother is unimportant. What is interesting is that heavy drinking could release a 'beast in the jungle', of whose existence he was normally unaware.

I have known a number of alcoholics—most of us have—but I can recall only two cases in which I had the sense of an underlying mystery, or at least, of a problem to be solved. One was a young farmer, whom I have known for years: a serious, hardworking man, who listens to music and reads poetry in his spare time. I had not seen him for about a year when he called on me one day. I offered him a glass of wine, but he refused. Knowing that he was not a heavy drinker, this did not surprise me. But he accepted an invitation to supper, and when the food came in, I again offered him a glass of wine; again, he refused. I asked: 'Afraid of becoming an alcoholic?' To my amazement, he said 'Yes'; he said it so seriously that I knew he wasn't joking.

He told me how it had come about. On cold winter mornings, he was up at five o'clock, calling in the cows for milking; he had done three hours' work before he went in for breakfast. One particularly dreary morning, he picked up a bottle of vodka from the sideboard and took a swallow before he went out to do the milking. It produced a pleasant glow, and the three hours went by more quickly than he had ever known them. The morning 'mouthful' of vodka against the cold became a habit. After breakfast, he often felt sleepy, but another swig of vodka remedied that. In order that his wife should not notice, he replaced the depleted vodka bottle, and at the same time bought a half-pint flask, which was easier to carry in his pocket. And it was when he was replacing this for the fourth or fifth time that he realised that he had become dependent on it, and was drinking a bottle a day. He said it came as a shock, because until then, he had been certain he was in control of his drinking; it was merely a matter of warming up on snowy mornings. For a while he tried to give it up without telling anyone; when it became obvious that he was losing the battle, he told his wife, and took medical advice. It was a slow, miserable struggle, in the course of which he joined Alcoholics Anonymous; eventually, he stopped drinking entirely. He drank water with his supper as he told me the story.

I suppose that what struck me as so puzzling was he seemed to me in no way the alcoholic type; young, happily married, intelligent. And here, I think, lies the key to the problem. He was a university graduate. The impulse that drove him to become a farmer was a kind of Whitmanesque romanticism about nature and the outdoor life. He has become a highly successful farmer, and apparently has no complaints about his choice. But milking cows and making hay is not the spiritually satisfying experience that Rousseau and Whitman and D. H. Lawrence seem to believe. It makes no real demand on the intelligence. And so a deep but unacknowledged frustration begins to build up, unrecognised by the conscious self; it becomes, in effect, a second personality, watching its chance of escape. . . .

The most remarkable alcoholic I have ever known was also one of the most remarkable men I have ever known. Negley Farson is one of the great travel writers; his autobiography, *The Way of a Transgressor*, must rank among the hundred best books of the twentieth century. In 1956, I drove down to Devon to meet him, with his son Dan and the late Kenneth Allsop. He was a great bear of a man, with a personality like a volcano: a non-stop talker, but also a very exciting talker; everything seemed to interest him. At dinner, while we drank wine, he drank water. His wife Eve explained without embarrassment that he was an alcoholic, and that if he touched a single glass, he went on drinking until he had to be put to bed. So he seldom drank. And when he did, he drank for two or three days, spent a week recovering, then stayed on the wagon for another month or so.

He told me one day how he became an alcoholic. When he started life as a journalist, he worked on the news desk, and had to take down stories as fast as they came in on teletype machines. He said that after two or three hours of this, working at top speed, he would hand over to his relief, stagger into the bar next door, and swallow two large whiskies just to unwind. After that, he heaved a sigh of relief and felt human. But after drinking at that speed, he found it difficult to return to a more leisurely pace. Besides, when he was drinking he turned into a sort of dynamo; stories about the past came pouring out of him. As he drank, he talked, and as he talked, he drank. He says in *A Mirror for Narcissus*: 'When I am drunk I will make even a lamp post stop and listen to me.'

His capacity was certainly incredible. One day when I was staying at The Grey House, near Woolacombe, he started to drink at lunchtime, and finished a bottle of whisky. Eve had hidden the rest of the booze in the house. He asked me if I had anything to drink in my room. I had: half a bottle of vodka, and half a bottle of gin. No doubt I should have lied and said I had nothing; but Negley wasn't the sort of person you could lie to. So I produced them, and watched him drink his way through both of them as he talked to me. The mixture seemed to have no ill-effect, and he was still talking, enthusiastically and lucidly, when he noticed he had emptied both bottles, and went out to search for more. . . .

One day in London, he invited me for lunch. I arrived around midday. He opened a bottle of whisky, and in less than an hour, we'd finished it—Negley drinking most of it. We then went into Soho and drank burgundy with lunch. Then we went back to his house, and he opened another bottle of whisky; before I left him at half past four, he had finished it.

The mystery of his alcoholism fascinated me, and gradually, I think, I came to understand it. The key lies in his travel books. He was obsessed by travel for the same reason that Casanova was obsessed by seduction, or Conrad by the sea. He possessed that curious romantic longing described by Rupert Brooke

. . . that fills
The soul with longing for dim hills
And far horizons. . . .

The appeal of his books is very like that of Hemingway's: they seem to breathe a smell of far-away places. He gives his reader the feeling that here is a man who has lived his life up to the hilt, as every desk-bound clerk dreams of living it. And in spite of his success and his happy marriage, this kind of romanticism could never be fully satisfied by the real world. He had a longing for a certain kind of freedom: the freedom he achieved as a roving foreign correspondent, or crossing the Caucasus in midwinter with a tent—a feat the natives assured him was impossible. He had a natural instinct for being in the places where the news was being made. He was actually in the Red Square in Moscow when the Revolution broke out in 1917. He was present at the arrest of Gandhi, and his story was a world exclusive. And when I knew him, he was living in one of the most beautiful spots in North Devon, overlooking the sea from a cliff top. But he still felt stifled. He talked about his past to maintain contact with it; but as he talked, I often felt that he wasn't in contact with it; these were only words that tried to recall it. But when he drank, he began to glow; you could see that the events became *real*. He was like a car that performs badly until it has been driven for half an hour; the alcohol brought his engine up to the right temperature. I have seen him achieve the same excitement without alcohol, when he was carried away by what he was describing; but a bottle of whisky was an easier and surer way of doing it. It was not a matter of chemical dependency, but the need of consciousness to widen its boundaries. This was recognised by a psychiatrist whom he consulted about his alcoholism. After a long analysis, the doctor said: 'Keep your alcoholism. If I cure it, I may also cure you of your talent.'

I am arguing that the usual view of alcoholism—as a disease—is incorrect, and that even the psychological theories get their emphasis wrong. It is a kind of despair that produces alcoholism: not the alcoholism, despair. Hemingway was a potential alcoholic all his life because he felt that life is fundamentally brutal and meaningless. While his work retained its imaginative tension, he stopped short of alcoholism; when his pessimistic philosophy led him into a *cul de sac*, he slid into alcoholism. American writers seem particularly prone to it, as Upton Sinclair, a rigid teetotaller, has pointed out. Jack London's early years were spent in incredible hardship and suffering, working for fourteen hours a day at labouring jobs that paid barely enough to live on. It turned him into a socialist and a writer. But even his socialism was basically pessimistic; he saw the world split into warring camps of brutal, inhuman capitalists and noble, oppressed workers; and his book *The Iron Heel* is as paranoid as Orwell's *1984*. So he drank himself into a feeling of pointlessness, then committed suicide.

Upton Sinclair cites London's example—and a dozen others —to prove that alcohol is a social evil, whether taken in large or small quantities. This argument strikes me as crude and simplistic—whether advanced by Sinclair or John Wesley or Andrew J. Volstead or Bernard Shaw. In its simplest form, it states that alcohol is a drug and a poison, and that its use is therefore immoral; society only tolerates it out of moral blindness. In fact, society recognises that when alcohol is used reasonably, its use is no more immoral than that of music or poetry. The difference is that while these act as stimulants to the imagination, alcohol only creates the conditions that allow imagination to expand and flourish.

This view receives confirmation from the findings of the psychologist Abraham Maslow. Maslow came to the conclusion that people become alcoholics because they are more sensitive and intelligent than the average; when faced by obstacles, the imagination works to their disadvantage; they concede defeat too easily. Because they drink in a mood of defeat, the drink only increases the depression. Maslow's colleague, Hoffer, cured alcoholics by giving them a dose of a psychedelic drug—to produce a more powerful lift than alcohol—and then, in this state of heightened sensitivity, giving them aesthetic experiences by means of music or poetry or colours blending on a screen. There was a cure-rate of more than seventy-five per cent; and the reason should be fairly clear. The intense upsurge of delight produces a feeling of optimism, and the recognition that this optimism is *justified*: that the world *is* a more meaningful and beautiful place than we usually recognise in everyday consciousness. The vicious circle of despair, pessimism and guilt is broken. Maslow argues that the alcoholic sees himself as a miserable, passive creature, perpetually on the defensive against *la force des choses*, the weight of the material world. Hoffer's experiment cured alcoholics by revealing to them that man possesses curious inner powers that give him the final advantage over things. These powers only work when they are summoned. Passivity and pessimism cause them to fall into disuse. Alcoholism is fundamentally a self-induced paralysis of the imagination, and a misguided protest against the fate that is responsible for the paralysis.

I have a theory which, if true, constitutes the most powerful argument in favour of alcohol. I have to admit that I am not wholly convinced by it; but it is plausible, and will make a fitting conclusion to this book. Biologists have not explained satisfactorily why man's evolution has been so much faster than that of any other living creature. He has changed more in thirteen thousand years than the horse in thirteen million—or than the shark in a hundred and fifty million. But the most startling change has occurred in the past ten thousand years—a mere blink of the eyelid in terms of evolution. In that time, man has changed from a creature who was little more than an intelligent chimpanzee into Rodin's thinker. Could it be entirely coincidence that this change has taken place since man discovered how to ferment alcohol, about 8000 B.C.?

The speculation occurred to me when I came across a reference in Virgil's *Georgics* to 'the white wine of Mareotis'. I had heard of this Mareotis in Yeats's poem *Under Ben Bulben*:

> Swear by what the sages knew
> Round the Mareotic Lake.

What was this Mareotis that provided a home for sages? I tracked down a reference in Philo Judaeus, who wrote: 'They [the Gnostic brotherhood] made their abodes outside the walls, in woods or enclosed lands in pursuit of solitude, not to indulge any feeling of churlish dislike to their fellow men, but from a knowledge that continual contact with people of dissimilar dispositions to their own is unprofitable and harmful.' He goes on to describe the 'therapeutic land' to which the most highly advanced hermits came, 'a spot exceedingly well adapted for the purpose, perched on a fairly high plateau overlooking Lake Mareotis, immediately south of Alexandria, in a most favourable situation both for security and mildness of climate. The mildness of temperature is due to the continual breezes sent up by the lake, which opens into the sea, and from the proximity of the open sea itself. The breezes from the sea are light, while those from the lake are heavy, and their combination produces a most healthy atmosphere.' What better combination: healthy atmosphere, mild climate, sea breezes—and, to act as a catalyst, the light and fragrant wine of Mareotis, mentioned by Virgil? The result: those profound meditations on the human and the divine, the visible and the invisible, that became the basis of the mystical Kabbalah.

Everyday life has always been hard; it still is for the majority of human beings. It is easy to understand how man came to develop the spear, the plough, the millstone; but difficult to understand how he came to create anything so irrelevant to everyday life as poetry, philosophy, mathematics. I would seriously suggest that the answer is: alcohol, with its curious power to release the mind. In that neglected metaphysical novel *Kater Murr* (which is narrated by a tomcat), E. T. A. Hoffman remarks that 'our flight is often hindered by leaden weights that we cannot identify, nor do we know where they come from, or who attached them.' And, later: 'Every man really has an innate inclination to fly, and I have known serious and respectable people, who in the late evening, fill themselves with champagne as a gas for ascending to the heights, as balloon and passenger at the same time.' Hoffman is a humorist, but I suspect that he has here stumbled on an important truth. It is, I agree, conceivable that philosophers and poets would have evolved without the aid of wine—young men fall in love and enjoy spring mornings; thoughtful men fall into meditation, as they sit on a fence and stare at the sunset. But surely our evolution would have been much slower without this instantaneous lightener of burdens? Wine creates detachment, a sense of potentiality, the 'worlds of If'; and this, in turn, creates optimism and courage—the prime necessity for evolution.

If my speculation is correct, then there is an important footnote to be added to the scientific definitions of man. He is not only *homo sapiens* and *homo faber*, the social animal, the tool-making animal; he is fundamentally *homo vinens*—the wine-making animal.

SELECTED BIBLIOGRAPHY

Selected Bibliography

Allen, H. Warner, *A History of Wine*, Faber & Faber, 1961

Barnard, Alfred, *The Whisky Distilleries of the United Kingdom*, David & Charles Reprints, 1969

Barzini, Luigi, *The Italians*, Hamish Hamilton, 1964

Brett, Gerard, *Dinner is Served*, Rupert Hart-Davis, 1968

Carter, Youngman, *Drinking Bordeaux*, Hamish Hamilton, 1966

Carter, Youngman, *Drinking Burgundy*, Hamish Hamilton, 1966

Churchill, Creighton, *The World of Wines*, Collier Books, New York, 1967

Croft-Cooke, Rupert, *Wine and Other Drinks*, Collins, 1962

Daiches, David, *Scotch Whisky*, André Deutsch, 1969

Doughty, Brian, *A Guide to Good Wine*, Abbey Library, 1970

Grossman, Harold J., *Grossman's Guide to Wines, Spirits, and Beers*, Charles Scribner's Sons, New York, 1955

Hallgarten, S. F., *Rhineland Wineland*, Elek Books, 1955

Healy, Maurice, *Stay Me with Flagons*, Michael Joseph, 1963

Hedrick, U. P., *Grapes and Wines from Home Vineyards*, Oxford University Press, 1945

House and Garden, *Wine*, Special Edition

Hyams, Edward, *Dionysus: A Social History of the Wine Vine*, Thames & Hudson, 1965

Jacquelin, Louis & Poulain, René, *The Wines and Vineyards of France*, Paul Hamlyn, 1962

James, Walter, *A Word Book of Wine*, Phoenix House, 1959

Johnson, Hugh, *The World Atlas of Wine*, Mitchell Beazley, 1969

Johnson, Hugh, *Wine*, Nelson, 1966

Leedom, William S., *The Vintage Wine Book*, Vintage Books, New York, 1963

Lichine, Alexis, *Encyclopedia of Wines and Spirits*, Cassell, 1967

Lockhart, Sir Robert Bruce, *Scotch: The Whisky of Scotland in Fact and Story*, Putnam, 1966

Lucia, Salvatore, P., M.D., *A History of Wine as Therapy*, J. B. Lippincott, New York, 1963

Marrison, L. W., *Wines and Spirits*, Penguin Books, 1963
Massee, William E., *Wines and Spirits*, Bramhall House, New York, 1961
Melville, John, *Guide to California Wines*, Nourse, San Carlos, California, 1960
Penning-Rowsell, Edmund, *The Wines of Bordeaux*, Michael Joseph, 1969
Postgate, Raymond, *The Plain Man's Guide to Wine*, Michael Joseph, 1962
Rainbird, George, *The Subtle Alchemist*, Michael Joseph, 1973
Ray, Cyril, *The Gourmet's Companion*, Eyre and Spottiswoode, 1963
Ray, Cyril, *Lafite*, Peter Davies, 1968
Redding, Cyrus, *A History and Description of Modern Wines*, Bohn's Library, 1849
Saintsbury, George, *A Last Vintage*, Methuen, 1950
Saintsbury, George, *Notes on a Cellar-Book*, Macmillan, 1963
Schoonmaker, Frank, *Encyclopedia of Wine*, Nelson, 1967
Schoonmaker, and Marvel, *American Wines*, Duell, Sloan & Pearce, New York, 1941
Shand, P. Morton, *Bacchus*, Kegan Paul, Trench, Trubner, 1927
Shand, P. Morton, *A Book of French Wines*, Jonathan Cape, 1960
Sichel, Allan, *The Penguin Book of Wines*, Penguin Books, 1965
Simon, André L., *A Wine Primer*, Michael Joseph, 1962
Simon, André L., *The Blood of the Grape*, Duckworth, 1920
Simon, André L., *Wines of the World*, McGraw-Hill, 1967
Veronelli, Luigi, *The Wines of Italy*, McGraw-Hill, 1964
Waugh, Alec, *In Praise of Wine and Certain Noble Spirits*, Cassell, 1959
Waugh, Evelyn, *Wine in Peace and War*, Saccone & Speed, 1949
Younger, William, *Gods, Men and Wine*, Michael Joseph, 1966
Yoxall, H. W., *The Wines of Burgundy*, Michael Joseph, 1968

INDEX